A brilliant exposition replete with cultura͏̈
Easy to read and follow so that, Jonah-lik͏̈
to the commands of our Lord who patientl͏̈

.. Lee, PhD
President ͏̈ ͏̈n Church History,
Torch Trinity Graduate ͏̈versity, Seoul, South Korea

Dr. Rosa Shao's commentary on the book of Jonah highlights the ways in which the prophet said "no" to God in order to encourage us instead to say "yes" to God without reservation. Her deep understanding of the text of Jonah combined with her detailed accounts of Christian experience in the Asian context have the potential to move Asian believers to say "yes" once again to God and to obey him in extending his abundant grace among all the nations of the world.

Joel F. Williams, PhD
New Testament Book Review Editor,
Journal of Evangelical Theological Society
Professor of New Testament Studies,
Biblical Seminary of the Philippines, Manila, Philippines

Asia Bible Commentary Series

JONAH

GLOBAL LIBRARY

Asia Bible Commentary Series

JONAH

Rosa Ching Shao

General Editor
Federico G. Villanueva

Old Testament Consulting Editors
Yohanna Katanacho, Tim Meadowcroft, Joseph Shao

New Testament Consulting Editors
Steve Chang, Andrew Spurgeon, Brian Wintle

© 2019 by Rosa Ching Shao

Published 2019 by Langham Global Library
an imprint of Langham Publishing
www.langhampublishing.org

Langham Publishing and its imprints are a ministry of Langham Partnership

Langham Partnership
PO Box 296, Carlisle, Cumbria, CA3 9WZ, UK
www.langham.org

Published in partnership with Asia Theological Association

ATA
QCC PO Box 1454–1154, Manila, Philippines
www.ataasia.com

ISBNs:
978-1-78368-645-2 Print
978-1-78368-691-9 ePub
978-1-78368-692-6 Mobi
978-1-78368-693-3 PDF

Rosa Ching Shao has asserted her right under the Copyright, Designs, and Patents Act, 1988 to be identified as the Author of this work.

All rights reserved. No part of this publication may be reproduced, stored in a retrieval system, or transmitted in any form or by any means, electronic, mechanical, photocopying, recording, or otherwise, without the prior written permission of the publisher or the Copyright Licensing Agency.

Unless otherwise stated, Scripture quotations are from the New International Version, copyright © 2011. Used by permission. All rights reserved.

Scripture quotations marked RSV are from Revised Standard Version of the Bible, copyright © 1946, 1952, and 1971 National Council of the Churches of Christ in the United States of America. Used by permission. All rights reserved.

Scripture quotations marked ESV are from The Holy Bible, English Standard Version® (ESV®), copyright © 2001 by Crossway, a publishing ministry of Good News Publishers. Used by permission. All rights reserved.

British Library Cataloguing in Publication Data
A catalogue record for this book is available from the British Library.

ISBN: 978-1-78368-645-2

Cover & Book Design: projectluz.com

Langham Partnership actively supports theological dialogue and an author's right to publish but does not necessarily endorse the views and opinions set forth and works referenced within this publication or guarantee its technical and grammatical correctness. Langham Partnership does not accept any responsibility or liability to persons or property as a consequence of the reading, use, or interpretation of its published content.

TO

Jane Chiong, sister in the Lord,
who never ceases to pray with me about
my personal calling to full-time service to God;

Joseph, my husband,
who brings out the best in me;

our children,
Jathniel and Rissah
Ruth and Daniel, with granddaughter Abigail
Reuelle and Matthew,
who keep me going amid both sunny and stormy days
with their endless cheers and prayers.

CONTENTS

Commentary

Foreword xi
Series Preface xiii
Author's Preface xv
List of Abbreviations xvii
Introduction 1
Commentary on Jonah 21
Selected Bibliography 83

Topics

Comparing the Biblical Jonah with the Qur'anic Version 18
Natural Calamities and Patron Saints 29
Is It a Whale or What? 37
Singing Out in Troubled Times 42
The God of Second Chances 52
Modern-Day Jonahs and Mass Conversions 61
Is God Playing Games with His People? 74
When Suicidal Thoughts Loom 76

FOREWORD

It is a special delight to commend to a wide-reading audience Dr. Rosa Shao's delightful commentary on the book of Jonah, for it has been my privilege to know her and her work in teaching for well over thirty years at the Biblical Seminary of the Philippines. I had also been the graduate teacher of her husband at Trinity Evangelical Divinity School in Deerfield, Illinois, some forty years ago.

Dr. Rosa Shao has produced at one and the same time a scholarly work – with appropriate critical references to the Hebrew text, where such references greatly enhance the understanding of the meaning of the book of Jonah – as well as providing useful illustrations taken from the fields of psychology and pastoral ministries. She has brought her dual achievements in the areas of biblical exegesis and clinical psychology to the writing of this commentary.

This commentary has been especially successful in being biblically accurate with regard to the culture of Jonah's day, as well as contextually relevant to our own day. Rosa is to be commended for the strong archaeological background she has been able to bring out in this text as well as for her great discussions on theology. Her illustrations from everyday life are likewise special gems that will endear this book to so many of her readers.

I strongly urge the use of this commentary not only within the Asian context, for which its contents set it forth as being beautifully distinctive, but also for the church at large around the world. The message of how God sent his messenger Jonah to Assyria, the land of Israel's enemy, but unfortunately, this messenger fled in the opposite direction and gave a silent but complete "no" to God's call, is contrasted with the love of God who gave this failing servant of his a second chance. Many who have been disobedient to the call of God for one reason or another, will take enormous comfort and encouragement from God's gracious offer of a second chance.

Walter C. Kaiser, Jr.,
President Emeritus,
Gordon-Conwell Theological Seminary,
Hamilton, Massachusetts, USA

SERIES PREFACE

In recent years, we have witnessed one of the greatest shifts in the history of world Christianity. It used to be that the majority of Christians lived in the West, but Christians are now evenly distributed around the globe. This shift has implications for the task of interpreting the Bible from within our respective contexts, which is in line with the growing realization that every theology is contextual. Thus, the questions that we bring into our reading of the Bible will be shaped by our present realities as well as our historical and social locations. There is a need therefore to interpret the Bible for our own contexts.

The Asia Bible Commentary (ABC) series addresses this need. In line with the mission of the Asia Theological Association Publications, we have gathered evangelical Bible scholars working among Asians to write commentaries on each book of the Bible. The mission is to "produce resources that are biblical, pastoral, contextual, missional, and prophetic for pastors, Christian leaders, cross-cultural workers, and students in Asia." Although the Bible can be studied for different reasons, we believe that it is given primarily for the edification of the Body of Christ (2 Tim 3:16–17). The ABC series is designed to help pastors in their sermon preparation, cell group or lay leaders in their Bible study groups, and those training in seminaries or Bible schools.

Each commentary begins with an introduction that provides general information about the book's author and original context, summarizes the main message or theme of the book, and outlines its potential relevance to a particular Asian context. The introduction is followed by an exposition that combines exegesis and application. Here, we seek to speak to and empower Christians in Asia by using our own stories, parables, poems, and other cultural resources as we expound the Bible.

The Bible is actually Asian in that it comes from ancient West Asia, and there are many similarities between the world of the Bible and traditional Asian cultures. But there are also many differences that we need to explore in some depth. That is why the commentaries also include articles or topics in which we bring specific issues in Asian church, social, and religious contexts into dialogue with relevant issues in the Bible. We do not seek to resolve every tension that emerges but rather to allow the text to illumine the context and vice versa, acknowledging that we do not have all the answers to every mystery.

Jonah

May the Holy Spirit, who inspired the writers of the Bible, bring light to the hearts and minds of all who use these materials, to the glory of God and to the building up of the churches!

Federico G. Villanueva
General Editor

AUTHOR'S PREFACE

A few years ago, I received an email from the Asia Theological Association (ATA) looking for writers for the book of Jonah. It stirred my interest to revisit my journey with the prophet Jonah. Nearly thirty-nine years ago, I had worked on an analytical key and exegetical commentary on Jonah, in partial fulfillment of the required degree in Master of Divinity in Biblical Studies at the Biblical Seminary of the Philippines. Surely it would be exciting to reenter the experience of this runaway prophet and upgrade my understanding of his message years after the effort on my thesis?

When the ATA tasked me with writing the commentary on Jonah, I found myself thinking of Jonah with the fish. A family visit to the Cincinnati Zoo came to mind, evoking fond memories of our then two-year-old son, afraid to go into the aquarium center because he had heard from his Sunday school teacher that a big fish had swallowed Jonah! I would soon reexamine how both God's tenderness and toughness could be seen in the provision of the fish and how the emotion of fear is so very real, even to a toddler.

Revisiting the account of Jonah also stirs my burden for lost souls. I reflect on the thousands of migrants fleeing their own troubled lands, seeking asylum and safe haven across the Mediterranean Sea as well as over barbed gates and walled borders. I had once stood at a resort in Antalya, Turkey, overlooking the vast Mediterranean Sea, and pictured Jonah taking a ship through Joppa to go to Tarshish – a little like those migrants escaping from a distressed homeland, except that Jonah was taking flight from God himself. A five-foot fish statue hangs beside a tree near the very shore where Jonah once set foot, and my interest in Jonah was rekindled, knowing I could be standing where Jonah himself had once stood. It is a timely endeavor to reconsider the book's missionary message in the light of so many boat people around us – are they not also treasured by our Lord God? How do we discern God's call to their needs in view of our increasing, yet also shrinking, global village?

The book of Jonah is short, simple, and succinct, but its simplicity is not tantamount to simplification. The narrative is packed with suspense, twists in the tale, and a continuous "wrestling" between Jonah and the Lord God. There is more than meets the eye in every chapter of the book.

The book of Jonah portrays how God deals with his servant in a personal way. Every servant of the Lord encounters some disturbance, and even disappointment, in doing God's work. Revisiting Jonah may help us realize that the Lord God cares more about his servants than about the tasks he assigns to them.

A poem by Bishop Ralph Cushman reminds me why I offer my life to serve God when I could make excuses and run away; this poem also challenges me to deepen my walk with God so that I may be able to last long and stay faithful in his ministry. It is titled *I Met God in the Storm*.[1]

> I met God in the storm
> Where he found me all forlorn;
> And he put his arm around me,
> And I thank him for the storm.
>
> I met God in the dark,
> Where I wandered stiff and stark;
> And he caught my hand to guide me
> And I thank him for the dark.
>
> I met God in defeat
> Where he followed my retreat
> With a vision of new conquest;
> Now I'm glad of that defeat.
>
> I met God by a grave
> Where he braced me to be brave
> But I failed and then he caught me;
> Yes, I thank him for that grave.
>
> I shall meet God when the night
> Overwhelms my flickering light;
> Then he'll lead me to the morning,
> Far away from cloud and storming,
> Where I'll praise him for the night.

---

1. Bishop Ralph S. Cushman in an unpublished dissertation, xii.

LIST OF ABBREVIATIONS

BOOKS OF THE BIBLE

Old Testament
Gen, Exod, Lev, Num, Deut, Josh, Judg, Ruth, 1–2 Sam, 1–2 Kgs, 1–2 Chr, Ezra, Neh, Esth, Job, Ps/Pss, Prov, Eccl, Song, Isa, Jer, Lam, Ezek, Dan, Hos, Joel, Amos, Obad, Jonah, Mic, Nah, Hab, Zeph, Hag, Zech, Mal

New Testament
Matt, Mark, Luke, John, Acts, Rom, 1–2 Cor, Gal, Eph, Phil, Col, 1–2 Thess, 1–2 Tim, Titus, Phlm, Heb, Jas, 1–2 Pet, 1–2–3 John, Jude, Rev

BIBLE TEXTS AND VERSIONS

Divisions of the canon
NT	New Testament
OT	Old Testament

Ancient texts and versions
LXX	Septuagint
MT	Masoretic Text

Modern versions
ESV	English Standard Version
KJV	King James Version
NASB	New American Standard Bible
NEB	New English Version
NIB	New Interpreter's Bible
NIV	New International Version

Journals, reference works, and series
ABC	Asia Bible Commentary
BDB	F. Brown, S. R. Drivers, C.A. Bricks, *A Hebrew and English Lexicon of the Old Testament*

CBQ	*Catholic Biblical Quarterly*
CTJ	*Calvin Theological Journal*
HALOT	*The Hebrew and Aramaic Lexicon of the Old Testament*
JAM	*Journal of Asian Mission*
JSOT	*Journal for Study of Old Testament*
NIBC	New International Biblical Commentary
NICOT	New International Commentary on the Old Testament
OTL	Old Testament Library
TOTC	Tyndale Old Testament Commentary
WBC	Word Biblical Commentary

INTRODUCTION

WHEN WE SAY "NO" TO GOD

As I thought about writing this commentary, I decided to find out how people today would remember Jonah and how they would describe him. In one of the faculty prayer meetings I was leading, I raised a simple question: "Have you ever said 'no' to God? If so, on what occasion?" Of the 60 percent who responded, almost three-fourths had said "no" to God. Some of these seminary faculty and staff had said "no" to God:

- when making a lifetime decision or choice such as dating someone or studying in a seminary;
- when dealing with personal sickness and repenting of sins; or
- when invited to join church activities and even to speak to God's people.

A common feature underlying all these situations was the requirement to deny self and leave one's personal plans and future in God's hands. This is scary, because what lies ahead is unknown and full of uncertainty. Although Jonah sees God as loving and compassionate, his running away from God says a loud "no!" Perhaps Jonah harbored fears of what God might have chosen to do through him and what this might have entailed for him.

I probed further: "What would happen if we say 'no' to God?" The replies poured in: "We would miss God's blessings," "We would encounter disappointment and lack of peace with God," "We would grieve the Holy Spirit and not be fruitful at work," and "Such disobedience to God will reap consequences." One person said, "The Lord will find a way to bring the person back into the sphere of his plan."

I followed up by asking, "Who then, could you recall, in the Bible, who has said 'no' to God?" There was hardly a pause before someone mentioned Jonah. The prophet Jonah is the main character in this book. His actions proclaim a loud "no" to God at the beginning of the narrative, and even his subsequent obedience is not a wholehearted "yes" but a grudging, reluctant compliance. Later, we hear his suicidal "no," as he asks God to let him die, and towards the end of his story, yet another "no" seems to emerge in his heated argument with God.

Jonah

The book of Jonah is both fun and fascinating. Jonah is one of the few people in the Old Testament who dared to say "no" to God. Although brief, Jonah's story is significant. Our Lord Jesus himself points to the "sign" of the prophet Jonah and draws a parallel between Jonah's time inside the fish and the Lord's own death and resurrection. Jesus said, to the skeptical Pharisees and teachers of the law: "A wicked and adulterous generation asks for a sign! But none will be given it except the sign of the prophet Jonah. For as Jonah was three days and three nights in the belly of a huge fish, so the Son of Man will be three days and three nights in the heart of the earth" (Matt 12:39–40).

Incidentally, of the twelve minor prophets in the Hebrew Bible, Jonah is the only one mentioned by name in the Qur'an. This is in the tenth chapter of the Qur'an, which has ninety-eight verses referring to Jonah. In Islam, Jonah is called *Dhul-Nun* (in Arabic ذو النون, meaning "The One of the Whale"). He is said to come from the tribe of Benjamin and is the son of Amittai. In Islamic tradition, Jonah (*Yunus* in Arabic, *Yunan* for Christian Arabs) is portrayed as a prophet who obeyed God and faithfully pronounced his message. While this story has some similarities to the account of Jonah in the Hebrew Bible, there are substantial differences. These will be discussed at the end of this introduction.

AUTHORSHIP

The book of Jonah does not identify its author. Below are arguments of biblical scholars for two possible views on authorship: (a) an unknown author; and (b) Jonah as the author.

Unknown Author

Scholars who reject the traditional view that Jonah wrote the book argue that (a) the book itself does not claim Jonah as its author and (b) the account is written in the third person. Furthermore, from a number of Aramaic expressions and the expression "king of Nineveh" used in the book, they argue that the author must have lived in late exilic or post-exilic times, probably in the Persian period.[1] This is because Aramaic vocabulary and usage infiltrated the Hebrew language during such periods. Thus Jonah, the son of Amittai (2 Kgs 14:25), could not be the author. Instead, these scholars suggest that an unknown writer compiled the story using Jonah's name. They also point out

---

1. John Drane, *Introducing the Old Testament*, 3rd ed. (Oxford: Lion Hudson, 2011), 191.

Introduction

that the missionary spirit expressed in this book was non-existent among the Jews even as early as the eighth century BC.

Jonah as the Author

The book itself does not cite Jonah as its author; but neither does it state that someone else has written it. The introductory formula (1:1) parallels that used in the books of Hosea, Joel, Micah, and Zephaniah, as well as other prophetic books about whose authorship there is little or no debate.

The objection that Jonah was written in the third person is weak. The introductory formula shows this to be a common practice, also found in the Pentateuch.

The argument for post-exilic authorship based on Aramaisms is rendered invalid for several reasons: As early as Hezekiah's reign, Aramaic was the diplomatic language that even the political and military rulers of Judah understood (2 Kgs 18:26; Isa 36:11). The early presence of Aramaic form and expressions is readily explained by the close proximity of Syria and Phoenicia to northern Israel, Jonah's native land. The thirty years of Syrian dominion (2 Kgs 13:1–7, 14–25) before the rule of Jeroboam II, together with the years of warfare for Israel's deliverance (2 Kgs 13:25; 14:23–28), would certainly have ensured that Aramaisms not only crept into the political, military, and business language, but also enriched the literature and religious language of northern Israel.

As to the absence of missionary spirit among the Hebrews, such a spirit has never been strong among them. This is seen not only as early as the eighth century BC but even in New Testament times. At Joppa, it took three visions from God before Peter really understood God's heart for the Gentiles and obeyed the call to preach to the Gentile Cornelius and his household.

JONAH: THE PROPHET WHO SAID "NO" TO GOD

From 2 Kings 14:25, we know that Jonah, son of Amittai, was born in Gath Hepher and was of the tribe of Zebulun. *Yonah*, his name in Hebrew, means "dove." His home was north of Nazareth, in Galilee. He lived in the reign of Jeroboam II (788–747 BC), probably between 800–780 BC. He prophesied about the victory and expansion of territory under Jeroboam II, king of Israel, during the war with the Syrians. This prophecy was fulfilled with the restoration of their ancient boundaries. Jonah's early ministry thus made him popular in Israel. Nevertheless, since Israel did not repent of her wickedness (2 Kgs 17:7–18), the nation rushed headlong into ruin.

Jonah

According to the book bearing his name, Jonah received a command from God to go to Nineveh and pronounce judgment against it on account of its wickedness. To many readers, the book of Jonah comes across as philosophical in nature and style – provoking them to think deeply as to the whys of such a challenging mission. Many unanswered questions arise in the readers' minds: What kind of fish swallowed Jonah? How was there a mass conversion at Nineveh based on the prophetic words of Jonah? What was the plant that seemed to grow so magically and what was the worm that caused it to wither? Why did Jonah rant and rave, and even wish for his own death? In spite of the sudden shifts in Jonah's many moods, God moves alongside the prophet as each stage of his mission unfolds. The last scene has God himself presenting a crucial question for Jonah's reflection: "You have been concerned . . . should I not have concern . . . ?"

In the end, though, readers are left with a sense of incompleteness, as if something is still unresolved – perhaps due to the absence of any mention of Jonah's final repentance. Some commentators consider this a hindrance to accepting Jonah's authorship. Those who do accept Jonah as the author argue that since only Jonah himself would have known the details of what transpired between God and Jonah, this supports the view of Jonah's authorship.[2] They hold that the book is Jonah's confession and that, having dared to reveal his own inner struggle, Jonah leaves God's response – his universal and unconditional love for human beings – as the final note.

DATE OF COMPOSITION

Most critical scholars date the book between 500 and 300 BC. They argue that (a) the book speaks of Nineveh as a city that no longer exists (3:3), (b) the phrase "king of Nineveh" does not refer to the king of Assyria, the one living in the Assyrian period, and (c) the concept of missionary universalism (as in Isaiah 40–66) is post-exilic.

Accepting Jonah's authorship, however, puts the date of writing in an earlier period, about 850–825 BC under Jeroboam's reign. As noted earlier, the use of Aramaic expressions is a strong argument for identifying Jonah with the prophet mentioned in 2 Kings 14:25. This Jonah was instrumental in enlarging Israel's borders in the days of Jeroboam II (793–753 BC).

---

2. Daniel Arnold, *Wrestling with God: Commentary on the Book of Jonah* (San Bernardino, CA: CreateSpace, 2014), 87–88; originally published as *Jonas: Bras de fer avec un Dieu de grâce* (Saint-Légier, Switzerland: Editions Emmaüs, 2004).

Introduction

The past tense of the verb "was" in Jonah 3:3 could only mean that the city had long since ceased to exist and not that Nineveh was not in existence at the time the book was written. The point is, it existed, but had only ceased to be so "exceedingly great." As for the references to the king of Assyria as the "king of Nineveh," the title truly reflects the authentic situation of the period. The later title is used when the Assyrian empire became a powerful kingdom.[3]

GENRE OF THE BOOK

The book of Jonah is one of the most controversial books when it comes to literary analysis. In the early centuries of the Christian era, it was relegated to fiction. Later, a tendency to oppose and deny anything supernatural hounded it, even seeking to put it totally out of the canon of Scripture. Throughout church history, biblical scholars have tended to regard the book as either history or fiction. But there have also been a wide range of suggestions falling somewhere in-between: fable, allegory, legend, parable, midrash, tragedy, novella, satire, or a didactic story.[4]

This wide variety of genres that has been suggested points to the book's complexity and sophistication. If classified as a fable, it would be taken as a narration not founded on facts, resting on a mythological, fairy-tale motif of a great fish swallowing and vomiting out Jonah. If viewed as an allegory, then every detail of the narrative would have to stand for something else in the real world; this would mean that almost anything could be interpreted as any one scholar wishes. If viewed as a legend, it would build on the main character as an exaggerated hero for the readers to emulate; it could then be related to history and overlaid with miracle and myth. Some scholars classify the book as a parable – a fictitious narrative with a moral message. Others consider it midrash – a commentary on a text such as 2 Kings 14:25; nevertheless, there is no scholarly agreement as to the OT passage on which the book should serve as a commentary.

It has also been pointed out that the book bears a striking resemblance to prophetic accounts, such as those focusing on the work of Elijah and Elisha.

---

3. John H. Walton, *Ancient Near Eastern Thought and the Old Testament: Introducing the Conceptual World of the Hebrew Bible*, 2nd ed. (Grand Rapids: Baker Academic, 2018), 28. Richard S. Hess, *The Old Testament: A Historical, Theological, and Critical Introduction* (Grand Rapids: Baker Academic, 2016), 641, argued that the title is not an anachronistic recreation of a fictional past.

4. Kevin J. Youngblood, *Jonah: God's Scandalous Mercy, Hearing the Message of Scripture: A Commentary on the Old Testament*, ed. Daniel I. Block (Grand Rapids: Zondervan, 2013), 36.

Jonah has been identified as the son of Amittai, the prophet from Gath Hepher (2 Kgs 14:25) and the book was accepted and read in antiquity as a prophetic book. It had also been included in the collection of the Jewish Tanakh known as "The Twelve." A prophetic account is a third-person narrative that recounts the remarkable achievements of God's prophets. It reveals the prophet's exemplary devotion to God, with a mission that expounds on God's divine attribute.

The book of Jonah has elicited diverse interpretations, stemming from conventional scholarly approaches – which take into consideration matters such as date, context, and authorial purpose – as well as popular approaches fueled by countless children's stories and picture books such as "Jonah and the Whale."[5]

This commentary treats the book of Jonah as a didactic historical narrative with a theological message for contemporary readers. There are many narratives under the Former Prophets division in the Hebrew canon. Jonah's narration falls into the genre of these prophetic accounts. A closer examination of the book shows a number of subgenres supporting the book's general purpose and style.[6] In any prophetic account, there is a commission narrative, where God appoints his prophet or servant for a specific task. Such prophetic accounts usually point to the prominent adventure of God's prophet, speaking of the prophet's remarkable action and attitude. At times these prophetic stories would also bring out the divine character of God. The inclusion of a poetic prayer-psalm in Jonah 2 conforms to the hymn patterns of many psalms (lament, thanksgiving, and even historical psalms) and is similar to many oracles of OT prophets, which include both prophecy and prayer (see Jer 14:1–9). The book's prophetic oracle in Jonah 3, albeit in just one sentence with five Hebrew words, conforms to known forms of prophetic utterance.

PURPOSE OF THE BOOK

The book of Jonah is heartwarming, written like the prophet's own biography, confessing both Jonah's flight and his "fight" with God. But its purpose is not simply to tell us a fascinating story! Jonah is didactic in nature; it has several inter-related purposes.

---

5. R. W. L. Moberly, "Educating Jonah," in *Old Testament Theology: Reading the Hebrew Bible as Christian Scripture* (Grand Rapids: Baker Academic, 2013), 182–183.
6. Youngblood, *Jonah: God's Scandalous Mercy*, 37.

Introduction

Message for Sinners and All Who Suffer: God Delivers

The book of Jonah proclaims God's readiness to deliver those in distress and to save all who repent of their evil ways and turn to him. The sailors on board cry out to God and experience his powerful deliverance, which leads to reverential worship. In his distress, Jonah cries out from inside the belly of the fish and experiences a dramatic deliverance as he is "vomited" onto dry land! The king of Nineveh urges all the people to "call urgently on God" and turn from their evil ways (3:8) – as they do so, they are delivered from destruction.

Message for the Jewish People: Rebuking Narrow-Minded Nationalism

The call of Abraham, the father of the nation, was not intended only to bless Abraham, or even just the nation of Israel. Rather, God intended the Hebrew people to be a blessing to the whole world: "I will bless those who bless you, and whoever curses you I will curse; and all peoples on earth will be blessed through you" (Gen 12:3). At Sinai, God said to Israel, "Now if you obey me fully and keep my covenant, then . . . you will be for me a kingdom of priests" (Exod 19:5–6). The nation of Israel was to become "priests" so that through them all peoples of the earth would come to a saving knowledge of the one, true God. Israel, however, while taking pride in its privileged status as God's chosen people, neglected the responsibilities that came with it and looked down on the Gentile nations instead of being a blessing to them.

Jonah's attitude toward the Ninevites echoes Israel's failure to discharge its duty of priesthood. As God's chosen messenger, Jonah should have functioned as a channel of blessing to the pagan city of Nineveh. But his silent "no" to God (in chapter 1) reveals his unwillingness to share God's message of mercy with Israel's enemies. One important purpose of the book is to address this deep-seated Jewish particularism and rebuke Jewish narrow-mindedness.

Message for All Humankind: Universality of God's Grace

God's universal plan for all nations is evident in the mission he entrusted to Israel (Exod 19:5–6). Israel, like Abraham (Gen 12:3), was to be a blessing to all peoples on earth. But while there were always individual Israelites who served as God's agents of blessing to non-Israelites (for instance, Abraham, Isaac, Joseph), the nation as a whole failed miserably in its prophetic vocation to bear God's light and truth to the nations around.

Jonah's story reflects, on a small scale, this failure of the nation at large. Jonah's suicidal "no" (in chapter 4) is an angry reaction to God's mercy towards the Ninevites. But the book's glorious finale (4:10–11) emphasizes an important purpose of the book: to show that God's gracious salvation, steadfast love, mercy, and compassion are not restricted to a select few or to a chosen nation, but are available for all people; and to impress upon God's people their responsibility to share this message of God's universal grace with everyone.

Message for God's Prophet

The books in the Minor Prophets contain God's messages to Israel, and sometimes to other nations, through his prophets. But the book of Jonah is, almost entirely, God's message to the prophet. In every chapter, God uses people, creatures, inanimate objects, and events to teach Jonah important lessons about who God is, how God works, and God's purposes for humanity.

THEOLOGICAL THEMES

The mere mention of the name "Jonah" probably recalls memories of Sunday school and the story of a whale swallowing a man. One would never imagine that a man swallowed by a big fish could come out alive and unhurt; even more extraordinary is Jonah, who not only survives, but proceeds to go to Nineveh and proclaim God's message. The book of Jonah demonstrates how God, the creator of our universe, is also the one who orchestrates events for his own sovereign purposes. Some of the theological themes running through the story are discussed below.

The Living God: Present and Powerful

The presence and power of God is seen or sensed in every chapter of this book. The creator God remains in control of all the events that unfold in the story of Jonah. Even though Jonah did not reveal his reason for running away from God, the eyes of the Lord followed Jonah wherever the prophet went. It is God who causes the wind to blow and the storm to rise. When the sailors, acting on Jonah's suggestion, throw him overboard, it is God who sends a fish to swallow Jonah. Later, it is God who orders the fish to vomit Jonah onto dry land. God is not merely ever present in the world he created, but always in control of everything. God sends his prophet an unspoken message: You can run, but you cannot hide. What happens to Jonah vividly portrays what might happen when we human beings say "no" to God.

When a successful mission at Nineveh causes Jonah to become angry, God has some interesting object lessons for his prophet, drawing on things from the created world: a leafy plant, a hungry worm, a scorching east wind, and the blazing heat. God's power is absolute, and over all creation – human beings, animals, plants, and even the weather. He is "the LORD God of heaven, who made the sea and the land," as Jonah attested to the pagan sailors at sea. At the beginning of time, the Creator had declared, "Let there be" (Gen 1:3, 6, 14) and it was so; now, in Jonah's story, it is as if God were saying: "Let there be a mighty whirlwind" and a strong great wind arose; "Let there be a sea monster" and a great fish came; "Let the plant spring up and show forth its shade" and a plant soon grew, and so on.

We can't run away from God because God is never far from any of us. Paul preached to the Athenians about this divine immanence using a familiar Greek quotation: "For in him we live and move and have our being" (Acts 17:28). To attempt to run away from God or his presence is like trying, unsuccessfully, to run away from our very self – and this can only end in chaos and confusion! As we read about how God deals with Jonah it is evident that he is not just a powerful force to be reckoned with, but a personal and living God.

The Listening God: Prayers and Pray-ers

God listens to prayerful utterances by anyone – believers or pagans – who cries out to him, in whatever their circumstances. The book of Jonah has prayers in every chapter. Chapter 1 opens with the pagan sailors, terrified by the raging storm and crying out to their own gods. But once they hear about Jonah's God, and learn the reason Jonah is running away from him, they plead for God's mercy and for release from accountability. As they reluctantly throw Jonah overboard, God calms the sea. God listens to the helpless cries of human hearts: "a broken and contrite heart you, God, will not despise" (Ps 51:17b). Prayer works!

In chapter 3, when Jonah pronounces God's judgment, the Ninevites take this prophetic warning to heart, calling upon God and repenting of their evil ways. Nineveh is spared as God withholds his judgment upon the city and its people. Again, prayer works!

In both these chapters, these prayers are uttered by pagan people. In the face of a universal crisis, all humankind stands helpless. And in their helplessness, people may cry out to the one who is greater, trusting God to "listen" to their pleas. When they experience deliverance from their distress, such people may recognize God's power and respond with adoration to his love.

In chapters 2 and 4, we find prayers of Jonah himself, on two very different occasions (2:1–9; 4:3, 8). In chapter 2, almost the whole passage contains what is popularly known as the "prayer of Jonah" and this prayer attests to Jonah's awakening readiness to assume the burdens of prophecy.

An important function of prayer is its effectiveness in changing the "pray-er" inwardly, even though circumstances may remain unchanged. Jonah's cry from the depths is not just a plea for help; surprisingly, it is uttered with a spirit of praise and thanksgiving. The God who "listens" to our every cry also gives the power that changes the pray-er from the inside – and that very change may also be an answer to prayer.

A look at these prayers and "pray-ers" (1:5, 14; 2:1–10; 3:8–10; 4:3, 8) in the book of Jonah shows that it is God's sovereignty that determines the outcome of every human petition. On two occasions, when pagans prayed, God delivered them. God listens to sincere pleas and knows what is best for those who have prayed. Jonah's desperate prayer-psalm was also received favorably and he was given a second chance to fulfill God's commission. However, prayer must be in accordance with God's will. In chapter 4, Jonah prays twice for his own death, but his wrongful requests are not granted. God's sovereign will is never bent to the blundering ways and sinful desires of human beings.

The Long-Suffering God: Patient with People

The central focus of the book is Jonah's relationship with God. When Jonah rebelled, God's justice seems swift as he orchestrates events to stop his runaway prophet. Yet, although God "sent" the storm that caused Jonah such distress (1:4), he also "provided" or "appointed" the big fish that saved Jonah (1:17).

Jonah knows that grace is the driving force behind God's actions and that God's justice is tempered with mercy. His own people, Israel, had experienced both the wrath and the compassion of God, both the justice and the mercy of God. God's justice demands destruction of the evil Ninevites; but if they will truly repent of their wickedness, God's mercy and grace abounds for them, just as it did for the Israelites and for Jonah himself. But Jonah does not *want* this amazing grace extended to the enemies of Israel. His sullen response, "I'm so angry I wish I were dead" (4:9), speaks of a stiff-necked resistance to the Lord God in the strongest of terms.[7] In fact, some scholars see this as the Yahweh-Jonah conflict, the dominant theme of which is Jonah's complaint that Yahweh God is too gracious, too merciful, too patient, and too loving, too prone to relent from punishment in the face of repentance.

---

7. Rob Barrett, "Meaning More than They Say: The Conflict between YHWH and Jonah," *JSOT* 37, no. 2 (2012): 245.

Introduction

As we pay close attention to Jonah's struggle with God, we see that God is both loving and long-suffering – towards the pagan sailors, the wicked Ninevites, and also his stubborn servant Jonah. The book of Jonah opens against the backdrop of the Yahweh-Nineveh conflict, which unveils the Yahweh-Jonah conflict, and finally we see the Yahweh-Humankind conflict showcased by God's patience despite Jonah's disobedience. This is God's loving kindness to all humankind; his grace that forgives and forgets. The Revised Standard Version is perhaps more accurate in speaking of God's "steadfast love." It is a blend of love and faithfulness that forms the core of the covenant. Covenant and *hesed* ("steadfast love") can be used synonymously: "I will make with you an everlasting covenant, my steadfast, sure love for David" (Isa 55:3b RSV). And in the end, this loving and long-suffering God silences his reluctant prophet with his patient rebuke: "And should I not have concern for the great city of Nineveh?" (4:11a).

RELEVANCE OF JONAH FOR THE ASIAN CONTEXT

As we consider the book of Jonah on the one hand and the Asian multi-cultural setting on the other, how do they relate? What is the relevance of Jonah's story for Asian readers today? Below are a few insights into Asian perspectives and the Asian mindset.

Asian Thinking

The scene at sea, with the sailors calling and crying out, each to their own God, is reminiscent of how many Asian people may shriek and scream to God in times of calamity. One Asian writer comments that the cries *Diyos ko* ("My God!") and *Hesus, tama na po* ("Jesus, enough please!") reveal our view of God.[8] Many people in Asia turn to God in their helplessness amid catastrophes from storms, typhoons, earthquakes, or tsunamis, asking *why* God would allow such disasters.

The Tagalog term *Bathala* means "the greatest one" or "the mighty one." The word *Bathala* is believed to have come from the Sanskrit *Bhattara Guru* or "the highest of the gods."[9] In Philippine mythology, he is the highest-ranking god of the ancient Tagalog people. Another name for *Bathala* is *Maykapal* or

---

8. Federico Villanueva, *Lamentations: A Pastoral and Contextual Commentary*, ABC (Carlisle: Langham Global Library, 2016), 5–6.
9. "*Bathala*, the Tagalog God," https://www.tagaloglang.com/bathala-the-tagalog-god/, accessed January 2, 2017.

Abba. He is considered the creator of all things, including the sea, the sky, the earth, and even the plants. Dangerous winds and disastrous storms are a perennial problem in the Philippine Islands. Since *Bathala* is considered the greatest and highest of all gods, when Filipino people experience being rescued from storms or shipwrecks, they would thank *Bathala* for saving them. They believe that *Bathala* is compassionate and grants favors to those who pay homage to him.

Bathala na ("it is in God's hands") is often shortened to *Bahala na* ("simply letting whatever happen"), a philosophy which may lead to a life lived either in resignation or in recklessness. On a positive note, the Filipinos seem able to accept whatever life has in store for them; even with a high percentage of people living in poverty, Filipinos are still reputed to be some of the happiest people in the world.[10] Yet, this attitude could also lead to irresponsibility – and the image of carefree Filipinos sitting idly under a coconut tree comes to mind.

Asian Doing

With over 86 percent of Filipinos being Roman Catholics, the Philippines is considered the only "Christian" Asian country. Christian beliefs have been combined with customary animistic practices over the years so that religion is often tainted with customs and ceremonies that call for harmony, forgiveness, and religiosity. Much of the time religion is closely connected to economic and political influences. With the collectivistic nature of the Filipino community and society, individual faith may not stand amid familial and relational influences which value family peace and congruence.

Repentance – in Hebrew *shub* (Jonah 3:8) – means "making a U-turn." The image is that of a person who turns away from old ways. It is a 180-degree turn from old ways to new, a change attested to by a transformed life. Moreover, true repentance calls for a final change – no more going back to old ways of doing things. But among many Asian believers, when God's mercy is lavishly highlighted, the focus tends to be on inner change without a corresponding emphasis on outward transformation. *Pasensiya*, the Tagalog word meaning patience, may connote merciful forbearing for someone. It is not equal to *pinatawad* ("forgiven" in Tagalog); yet it may imply forgiveness and long-suffering toward someone. It may indirectly express an expansive grace

---

10. Dharel Placido, "PH Third Happiest Country in the World – Gallup Survey," ABS-CBN News, https://news.abs-cbn.com/focus/01/02/18/ph-third-happiest-country-in-the-world-gallup-survey, accessed April 17, 2019.

towards the person who is remorseful or penitent. Such plea for *pasensiya* could even be valid for many occasions of transgression.[11]

Perhaps this is an instance of religious pluralism in Asian theology, where the spaciousness of God is emphasized so that other religious experiences and traditions embedded in the Asian geographic land may be embraced.[12] This is seen in the vast continent of Asia where more than 90 percent are non-Christian.

It is only as we give space for repentant people to change that we can see grace in action – as people gradually make a U-turn, leaving behind their evil ways and living out divine new ways. The relational distinctiveness of Christ's redemptive work on the cross stands out as unique and significant amid the pluralistic setting of Asian religions because it is only Christ who says: "Father, forgive them, for they do not know what they are doing" (Luke 23:34).

Asian Nationalism

Many writings that highlight God's universal love and mercy have criticized Jonah as the personification of a narrow-minded Jew; others blame Jonah for his nationalism and particularism. Jonah's anger and unrepentance over God's treatment of Nineveh is denounced, while Nineveh's humble repentance is applauded. God twice asks Jonah: "Is it right for you to be angry?" (4:4, 9); these writings do not give Jonah the legitimate right to be fuming.

Consider the historical context of the colonized Jewish people, invaded and oppressed by powerful nations such as Assyria. It seems inevitable, even natural, that God's people would have wrestled with the issue of God's justice. There have been some writers who empathize with Jonah's silence and anger. One such writer, Ryu, even regards Jonah's silence and anger as "a resistance on the part of the weak over against the rhetoric of the strong, which ignores unbalanced power structures in human relationships in the name of universalism."[13] Ryu will neither blame Jonah's anger nor openly praise God's love for all nations. He cites the continuing pain of the memories of his own country, Korea, after suffering aggression and atrocities from colonizers. He sees Jonah's stubborn refusal to celebrate God's universal love for Nineveh as a natural

---

11. Interestingly, there is even a local brand of cookies named *pasencia*, from *pasensiya*.
12. Sathianathan Clarke, "The Task, Method and Content of Asian Theologies," in *Asian Theology on the Way: Christianity, Culture and Context*, ed., Peniel Jesudason Rufus Rajkumar, ch. 1 (London: SPCK, 2012), 7–8.
13. Chesung Justin Ryu, "Silence as Resistance: A Postcolonial Reading of the Silence of Jonah in Jonah 4: 1–11," *JSOT* 34, no. 2 (2009): 198.

reaction – the oppressed people would not hide their anger upon seeing their oppressors redeemed by the God of the oppressed!

How does this attitude play out for us in the Philippines, where it is the colonizers themselves who brought the gospel to us? Philippine history shows that the Spaniards forced Christianity into our lands. However, it was the Spaniards who benefitted the most from Christendom under the Spanish regime. The friar lands, designated for the use of the church, constituted a scandal since the Filipinos were being robbed of their soil. Do we relate to Jonah's anger and silence in the way we articulate our pain and suffering under our colonizers?

Asian Shame

Shame is a sickness of the human soul. Kaufman defines shame as "the most poignant experience of the self by the self, whether felt in humiliation or cowardice, or in a sense of failure to cope successfully with challenge. Shame is a wound felt from the inside, dividing us both from ourselves and from one another."[14] Shame is an internalized, disturbing inner state that conditions every relationship in our lives, destroying self-esteem and leading to a kind of living death. It is different from both guilt and the feeling of guilt. Guilt says, "I've *done* something wrong," while shame says, "There is something wrong with *me*."

Religious shame is more pervasive in the social culture of Asian countries like China, Japan, and the Philippines. Shame is an emotion that includes the anxiety or fear of being disgraced or humiliated. Jonah knew, beforehand, that God was "a gracious and compassionate God, slow to anger and abounding in love" (4:2), and thus anticipated that God would relent from sending destruction upon the Ninevites, the enemies of the Israelites. When this outcome was finally realized, Jonah would have experienced shame, the shame that brings with it the fear of being looked upon with contempt by his own people, whose suffering he had dishonored by successfully warning their enemies against God's judgment. Jonah's actions saved their enemies from damnation. As if banging on heaven's door to make his shame-filled soul known to God, Jonah demanded, "Now, LORD, take away my life, for it is better for me to die than to live" (4:3). There is anger in Jonah's outrageous plea for death. One Chinese idiom expresses Jonah's raging shame as 老羞成怒 (*lao xiu cheng nu*), literally, "old shame turned anger."

---

14. Gershen Kaufman, *Shame: The Power of Caring*, 3rd ed. (Rochester, VT: Schenkman Books, 1992), vii–viii.

Introduction

In the Asian collectivistic culture, the shaming experiences of one's parents or government are often passed on to the next generation. The experience of shame may also lead to a kind of self-murder. For instance, the Japanese who does his country wrong may seek death by suicide rather than live with the pain of shame. Both Japan and Germany committed a great many atrocities in World War II. But while Germany has opted to openly and fully acknowledge their inhumanities, many Japanese textbooks do not even mention the atrocities committed by their own country and the facts have been altered to reflect Japan in a better light. The culture of shame underlies this inability to admit the wrongdoing.

Honor and shame are important themes in the Bible (1 Sam 2:7–8; Ps 62:7; 1 Pet 2:6–7; Rom 9:33; 10:11). When King Saul was wounded by Philistine archers, he chose to die by falling on his own sword. This was to safeguard his honor even in the midst of falling in shame at losing the war (1 Sam 31:4). Anthropologists have developed the idea of "shame cultures,"[15] and have found that some cultures place a higher priority than others on preserving honor and avoiding shame.[16]

STRUCTURE AND OUTLINE

The Intrigue of Jonah

The story of Jonah is told in a mere forty-eight verses. We can browse through it in less than ten minutes. Someone even calculated that the book of Jonah could be printed on half a page of a modern-day newspaper. Yet the whole story bubbles with life, action, and sharp, snappy dialogues. Both adults and Sunday school kids enjoy this story, and it is even familiar to the man on the street. Nevertheless, the book's brevity and simplicity should not be equated with a lack of complexity or depth. As the plot unfolds, the storyteller swiftly changes the backdrop of each scene, introducing twists and turns that keep readers on their toes as they strive to follow the fast-paced action.

Structure of the Book

The book of Jonah – with the exception of chapter 2, which is poetry – is the only prophetic book in the Bible that is written in narrative form. The prose

---

15. Andy Crouch, "The Return of Shame," *Christianity Today*, March 10, 2015, 37.
16. For a more detailed explanation of the shame factor in the Asian context, see Joseph Too Shao and Rosa Ching Shao, *Ezra and Nehemiah*, ABC (Carlisle: Langham Global Library, 2019).

narrative nature of the book is one of a kind, making it difficult to classify in terms of genre. (This issue on genre was addressed earlier in the book.)

The book of Jonah highlights God's abundant mercy toward a hostile people. With a hint of satire, the narrative draws out the exemplary proper response to God's word and mercy by the idolatrous Gentile sailors and the wicked people of Nineveh, rather than by God's commissioned prophet Jonah.

The repeated phase, "The word of the LORD came to Jonah" (1:1; 3:1) marks the two halves of the book. A closer look at the four chapters reveals a concentric or chiasmic structure. Each part has two main sections and each part also has a preface. The first and third chapters correspond to each other, as do the second and fourth chapters. In chapters 1 and 3, Jonah is placed in a situation where a group of pagans appeal to God for help; in chapters 2 and 4, Jonah is without human company and speaks with God alone. Jonah 1:3 highlights Jonah's disobedience to God, while 3:3 notes his obedience. Chapter 1, which narrates the sailors' reverence, is parallel to the later section which deals with the Ninevites' repentance (3:5–9). The demonstration of divine grace in 1:17 parallels 3:10; the former speaks of Jonah's relief, whereas the latter mentions the sparing of the repentant Ninevites, both under God's divine love. The following clearly shows the detailed double linear structure:

    A 1:1–2   The First Preface: God's First Call

        B 1:3–16   Jonah's Disobedience

            C 1:17–2:10 Jonah's Prayer and Praise

    A' 3: 1–2   The Second Preface: God's Second Call

        B' 3:3–10   Jonah's Obedience

            C' 4:1–11   Jonah's Dismay

Jonah's poetic song of praise in chapter 2 has three stanzas (verses 2–4; 5–7; 8–9); the chapter may also be viewed as consisting of two main parts: petition (verses 2–7) and thanksgiving praise (verses 8–9), which is in contrast to the prophet's complaint in chapter 4:1–3. Both these sections have almost the identical introduction, "Jonah [He] prayed to the LORD . . ." (2:1; 4:2). Ironically, the divine qualities that made Jonah sing praises to God are the very ones that would later cause him to grieve. In the final section (4:4–11), which is parallel to 2:10, God responds – with both his word and his works from nature – to his reluctant and ranting prophet.

Introduction

Outline of the Book
JONAH 1:1 – 2:10 THE FIRST COMMISSION FROM GOD

1:1–2 RECOGNITION OF THE PROPHET
- 1:1 Called by God
- 1:2 Commissioned to Preach against Nineveh

1:3–16 REBELLION OF THE PROPHET
- 1:3 Fleeing the Call of God
- 1:4–10 Fearing the Chaos at Sea
- 1:11–16 Facing the Consequences of Sin

1:17 – 2:10 REPENTANCE OF THE PROPHET
- 1:17 Rescued by God
- 2:1–9 Remembrance of God
    - 2:1–7 Praying to God
    - 2:8–9 Praising God
- 2:10 Relief for the Prophet

JONAH 3:1 – 4:11 THE SECOND COMMISSION FROM GOD

3:1–4 RECOMMISSIONING FROM GOD
- 3:1–2 Recommissioning of the Prophet
- 3:3–4 Response of the Prophet

3:5–9 REPENTING OF THE NINEVITES
- 3:5–6 Response of the Ninevites
- 3:7–9 Royal Decree of the King

3:10 RELENTING OF PUNISHMENT BY GOD

4:1–11 RAGING AGAINST GOD'S COMPASSION
- 4:1–2 Reproaching God
- 4:3–9 Requesting Death
- 4:10–11 Reproved by God

COMPARING THE BIBLICAL JONAH WITH THE QUR'ANIC VERSION

There are eight differences between the biblical account and the Qur'anic version of Jonah, and there is a vast difference in the emphases of the two accounts.[1] In the biblical account, God deals with his messenger, the prophet Jonah, in deeper and more personal ways, whereas in the Qur'an, the focus seems to be on gaining God's favor by crying to him in supplication as Jonah did when he was in distress. The biblical account portrays a disobedient Jonah, whereas in the Qur'an account, Jonah is depicted as an obedient prophet who goes directly to his place of assigned service. There is also a difference in the use of the prophet's name: the biblical account calls him Jonah, while in the Qur'an, the name of the prophet is Yunus, whose mission is to tell his people that there is a way out of destruction if only they have faith.[2]

Below are the eight differences:

(1) There is a difference in the emphasis of the commission of Jonah. In the biblical account, God commissions the prophet Jonah to preach against Nineveh – a foreign nation far from Israel, Jonah's own homeland – because their wickedness has come before God. In the Qur'an version, God calls the prophet Jonah to bring the message to his own people in Nineveh, telling them to stop their evil behavior and worship only one God, not many gods;

(2) There is a difference in the prophetic path of Jonah. In the biblical account, Jonah goes in an opposite direction, fleeing from God in a ship toward Tarshish. In the Qur'an, the prophet Jonah goes to Nineveh but the people refuse to listen to him and their conduct exasperates him; and so Jonah leaves them with a curse, saying that God would deal with them himself.

(3) The purpose of natural catastrophes is different. In the biblical account, Jonah found a ship and was sound asleep on the lower deck when God brought about a raging storm that threatened everyone on board. In the Qur'an, after Jonah leaves Nineveh the people see the sky changing into a fiery red blaze and realize that they are facing destruction under God's wrath. They all beg for God's forgiveness and God acknowledges their repentance and spares Nineveh from destruction. Thus, the people now hope that Jonah will return to them and teach them God's ways.

(4) There is a difference in the way Jonah ends up in the sea. In the biblical account, Jonah tells the sailors that if they throw him overboard the storm would stop. Reluctantly and fearfully the sailors do so. In

Introduction

the Qur'an, Jonah finds a ship to take him far away from his stubborn people. A great storm arises, and the passengers try to lighten the load by throwing things overboard. They, too, drew lots and the lot falls on Jonah. The passengers, who knew Jonah as a pious and righteous man, refuse to throw him into the sea. But when the lot falls on him again, Jonah knows the choice is God's and jumps into the sea and falls into the jaws of a giant fish.

(5) Why is Jonah in the belly of the fish? In the biblical account, God provides a big fish to swallow Jonah and the prophet is in the belly of the fish three days and three nights. From inside the fish, Jonah prays, calling upon the Lord for mercy, praising God for his deliverance, and making a thanksgiving vow. In the Qur'an, Jonah suddenly realizes that he is inside the belly of the fish (with no mention of the duration). He acknowledges his wrongdoing and bad behavior, and cries out to God: "None has the right to be worshiped but you, Oh God, glorified are you and truly I have been one of the wrongdoers!" (Qur'an 21:87).

(6) There is a difference in how Jonah ends up in Nineveh. In the biblical account, God commands the fish to vomit Jonah onto dry land, and Jonah gets a second chance to carry out his mission. Jonah obeys God and goes to Nineveh, where he proclaims God's message: "Forty more days and Nineveh will be overthrown." In the Qur'an, the angels heard Jonah crying in pain and praying inside the belly of the fish and approach God on his behalf. God remembers Jonah in his time of distress and commands the giant fish to eject Jonah on shore. Jonah continues to be in pain and repeats his supplication over and over again; God then provides a vine tree for Jonah's covering and for his food.

(7) There is a difference in the way Jonah handles his frustration and pain. In the biblical account, Jonah grows furious when he sees that God relented from destroying Nineveh. He pleads with God to let him die rather than see the deliverance of Nineveh. In the Qur'an, Jonah recovers from his physical wounds and pain, and returns to his people in Nineveh. The people welcome him and tell him how they had repented. Jonah stays with his people, teaching them to worship the one and only God.

(8) There is a difference in the focus of the gracious compassion of God for his creatures. In the biblical account, God speaks to Jonah and reasons with him about whether it is right for Jonah to be so angry as to demand his own death. God uses the plant to teach Jonah the sovereignty of the creator over his creatures, and to illustrate God's gracious compassion for all people. In the Qur'an, Jonah lives with more than one hundred thousand people in Nineveh. The moral

teaching of this account is patience under adversity by turning to God with sincerity. If one cries out to God in supplication, as Jonah did, God will hear and answer.

---

1. For the Yunus account in Qur'an, see Aisha Stacy, "Prophet Jonah," https://www.islamreligion.com/articles/2548/prophet-jonah/, accessed June 15, 2018.
2. Idris Tawfiq, "In the Belly of the Whale – The Story of Jonah," http://aboutislam.net/reading-islam/understanding-islam/in-the-belly-of-the-whale-story-of-jonah/, accessed June 15, 2018.

COMMENTARY

As I write, schools are closed in most cities of the Philippines due to the landfall of two cyclones circling around the archipelago. Last night, amid howling winds and non-stop rain, the weather station issued warnings and the news that classes would be suspended. The country weather bureau PAG-ASA announced that as of yesterday, September 11, 2017 4PM, typhoon "Lannie" had entered the Philippine Area of Responsibility while tropical depression "Maring" is due to set her mark by noon today.

Such news causes great fear, anxiety, tension, and emotional stress. People remain on red alert. But how much more frightening and dangerous when such bad weather is experienced while out at sea, with winds and waves battering mercilessly against one's sailboat or ship?

With these thoughts, we now consider the plight of Jonah as he set sail towards Tarshish. The narrative says: "Then the Lord sent a great wind on the sea, and such a violent storm arose that the ship threatened to break up" (1:4). What would happen to Jonah and the rest of the people on board that ship? What were they thinking and how were they feeling in the midst of that terrible storm?

JONAH 1:1 – 2:10
THE FIRST COMMISSION FROM GOD

The opening verses of the book of Jonah clearly state God's first commission to the prophet; and Jonah is identified as God's messenger. God commissions Jonah to go and preach against the great city of Nineveh in the east "because its wickedness has come up before me" (1:2). But Jonah takes off in the opposite direction, and boards a ship headed west. This spells trouble, not only for Jonah but also for the pagan sailors and other passengers on the ship (1:3–16). Jonah was tasked with a godly mission, but his silent "no" to God is a loud act of rebellion.

The Lord God sends a sudden storm to deal with his runaway messenger (1:4–10). As the wind and the waves grow increasingly fierce, chaos reigns on board, with the fearful pagan sailors crying out to their gods and making every effort to keep the ship afloat. Jonah, however, has gone below deck and is enjoying a sound sleep, seemingly unmindful of this great danger. The sailors draw lots to see who is responsible for this unexpected and terrible storm. Jonah is identified as the culprit and has to face the consequences. To his credit, Jonah does suggest that the sailors throw him overboard so that the sea will calm down. When all else fails they reluctantly, and fearfully, do so (1:11–16)!

Some interesting parallels in chapter 1:		
Hurling	The Lord hurls a wind (1:4a)	The sailors hurl Jonah (1:15a)
Wind	Raging storm (1:4b)	Raging sea grew calm (1:15b)
Prayer	Jonah urged to pray (1:6)	The sailors pray (1:14)
Accountability	Questioning Jonah (1:7–8)	Jonah admits (1:12)

1:1–2 RECOGNITION OF THE PROPHET

With only brief instructions from the Lord – specifying where to go, what to do, and why – Jonah responds with strong negative body language. He chooses a direction totally opposite to where the Lord wants him to go. Who was this prophet who dared take such a defiant course of action against the Lord God?

We are not told how God spoke to Jonah. Did this message of the Lord come to him through a dream, in a vision, or an audible voice?

1:1 Called by God

"The word of the LORD came to Jonah son of Amittai" (1:1). The narrative opens with the phrase "the word of the LORD came to Jonah."[1] Jonah has a mission from God. His call from God is introduced in similar manner to other prophetic books such as Hosea, Joel, Micah, and Zephaniah, each of which contain the same elements: the word from the Lord, addressed to a prophet.

Nothing is said about Jonah's family other than that he was the son of Amittai. Reference is also made to Jonah in 2 Kings 14:25. The root word of Amittai means "truth." So apart from meaning "dove," Jonah's name may also mean "the son of truth."

The phrase "the word of the LORD" appears in the Old Testament 438 times and is found at least 85 times in the historical accounts of the OT characters (Gen 15:1; Exod 9:20; Num 15:31; 1 Sam 15:10; 2 Sam 7:4; 1 Kgs 17:8; Jer 1:4, 11, 13; Ezek 3:16; Hag 1:3). Here, the coming of "the word of the LORD" affirms the authenticity of Jonah and the seriousness of God's divine calling upon him; the phrase also signifies that God is very much in control.

The narrative is quite open about Jonah's various "tantrums" because of the Lord God's commission. As each chapter develops, the twists and turns in Jonah's story depict a kind of wrestling match between the Lord God and his stubborn prophet Jonah. Upon hearing God's commission, Jonah does an about-face and flees from God's call. This is the first twist, seen in the prophet's silent "no" to God.

1:2 Commissioned to Preach against Nineveh

"Go to the great city of Nineveh and preach against it, because its wickedness has come up before me" (1:2). The urgency and the authority of God's commission to Jonah are evident in the imperatives *go* to Nineveh and *preach against* it. God means what he says. Nineveh was the largest city of Assyria at the time, but not the capital city as some earlier commentators thought. It only became the capital during the reign of Sennacherib (704–681 BC), more than half a century after the visit of Jonah.[2] Nineveh (modern-day Mosul,

---

[1]. In Hebrew, verse 1 begins with the word *wayehi*, literally "once there was/so it happened that."
[2]. Joshua J. Mark, "Nineveh: Definition," *Ancient History Encyclopedia*, https://www.ancient.eu/nineveh/, accessed November 6, 2017.

Iraq) had long been Israel's enemy. God's wrath was against Nineveh because of its history of violence and cruelty.[3] The prophet Nahum writes about the unending and unrepentant brutality of Nineveh against Judah, calling for God's divine judgment against the Ninevites. It is described as "the city of blood, full of lies, full of plunder, never without victims" (Nah 3:1). Nineveh is noted for arbitrarily killing captives, deceiving their subjects, and arrogantly oppressing the people of many nations.[4] Nothing is hidden before God. Just as God punished the twin cities Sodom and Gomorrah in the time of the patriarch Abraham, God decides to destroy the city of Nineveh because of its evil ways. Wicked is the word used to describe both Nineveh's situation and that of Sodom and Gomorrah (1:2; Gen 13:10, 13).

In Abram's time, God only informed him of the imminent destruction of Sodom and Gomorrah; Abraham was not instructed to proclaim judgment upon these cities. In Jonah's case, however, God not only informs the prophet of his divine judgment upon Nineveh but commissions Jonah to go to that very city to proclaim judgment against them.

Unlike Abram, Jonah did not want to bless Nineveh. Abraham's initial encounter with the king of Sodom (Gen 14) provides an interesting insight into God's call upon him, not only to bless him but also to make him a blessing to all the families of the earth (Gen 12:1–3). When Abraham learns that his nephew Lot has been taken captive by an alliance of four kings – who invade and defeat a local confederation of five kings (among which is the king of Sodom) – Abraham organizes a small army of allies and pursues the invaders. Abraham successfully recovers Lot and a large quantity of plunder. The king of Sodom tells Abraham, "Give me the people and keep the goods for yourself" (Gen 14:21). Abraham rejects this offer and daringly shows his full dependence on God, and not on any human kings, to become rich and great. On a later occasion, when God discloses to Abraham his plan to destroy the wicked cities of Sodom and Gomorrah, Abraham, probably with Lot in mind, intercedes with God to spare the righteous in Sodom (Gen 18:16–33).

---

3. Ray Vander Laan, "That the World May Know," https://www.thattheworldmayknow.com/assyrians/, accessed November 4, 2017. Archaeologists have uncovered many of these Assyrian records recounting victories and plunder. These are some of the chilling ways the Assyrians tortured their captives: flaying (cutting skin into strips and pulling it off a living victim); beheading; impaling (inserting a sharpened stake beneath the rib cage of a living victim, putting the stake into the ground so it stood erect, and leaving the victim until the stake pierced a vital organ causing the victim to die); burning people alive (especially babies and children); severing hands, feet, noses, ears, tongues, and testicles, and gouging out eyes.
4. Joseph T. Shao and Rosa C. Shao, *Joel, Nahum & Malachi*, ABC (Manila: Asia Theological Association, 2013), 81.

Through Abraham's prayerful requests, God spares Lot and his family from the destruction that comes upon Sodom and Gomorrah (Gen 19:29).

In other prophetic books of the OT, the Lord God told Isaiah, Jeremiah, and Ezekiel to proclaim judgment upon Israel and Judah, and even upon foreign nations. Many of these messages concluded with a final charge to the Hebrew people, encouraging them to wait and to be patient when they see the fleeting success of their enemies (Isa 13–25; Jer 46–50; Ezek 25–32). It is unlikely that these prophets ever actually set foot on those foreign lands against whom they announced God's divine judgment. Jonah is probably the only prophet whom the Lord God physically sent to preach his message of doom to a foreign people in a foreign land. Jonah is also the only prophet who rebels so outrageously against the call of God.

1:3–16 REBELLION OF THE PROPHET

The messenger of God acts contrary to the sender's instructions. God had said to go to Nineveh, which lies east, a journey entailing travel by land. Instead, Jonah set out for Tarshish in the west – the farthest possible location, from the Israelites' perspective – journeying by sea. While Jonah may not have verbalized a "no" to God, his actions spoke volumes. The action verb "go down" (*yarad*) is used three times with Jonah as the subject, underscoring his determination to defy the Lord.

1:3 Fleeing the Call of God

"But Jonah ran away from the LORD and headed for Tarshish. He went down to Joppa, where he found a ship bound for that port. After paying the fare, he went aboard and sailed for Tarshish to flee from the LORD" (1:3). This silent "no" is unbecoming of God's messenger. Spiritual giants like Moses, Gideon, and Jeremiah also tried to evade God's commission, partly due to their feeling of inadequacy, but also because they feared rejection and opposition from the people to the task assigned by God. At this point, the narrative is silent about the reason for Jonah's disobedience. He is running away from the Lord and heading for Tarshish (1:3) – his refusal to go to Nineveh is directly against the Lord God, but it is also indirectly against the Ninevites. The course of disobedience runs smoothly! Jonah experiences no problem in going down to Joppa and finding a ship to take him to Tarshish.

In the Hebrew text, the phrase "to Tarshish" is repeated three times in verse 3: "But Jonah rose to flee *to Tarshish* from the presence of the LORD. He went down to Joppa and found a ship going *to Tarshish*. So he paid the fare and went down into it, to go with them *to Tarshish*, away from the presence of the LORD" (1:3 ESV, italics mine). This underscores that Jonah is *not* going to Nineveh. Nineveh was on the east bank of the Tigris River, about 354 kilometers (220 miles) north of present-day Baghdad and over 805 kilometers (500 miles) northeast of Israel. On the other hand, Tarshish was an unknown locale, associated with a distant coastland somewhere in the western Mediterranean. It was the farthest place to which one could travel during that time. Today, we recognize it as a place in modern Spain that is directly opposite Nineveh. Instead of taking a journey by land, approximately 1,000 kilometers east of Israel, to go to Nineveh, Jonah takes a ship to Tarshish, located about 3,800 kilometers west of Israel. Jonah both resists and rebels against the divine call.

1:4–10 Fearing the Chaos at Sea

God's special mission for Jonah, his servant and prophet, is not to be thwarted. At the beginning of the narrative, when the word of the Lord came to Jonah, there does not seem to have been any sign of wind or rain. But as God deals with his runaway prophet, he "sent" (literally, "hurled") a great wind on the sea and a violent storm arose, endangering everyone in the ship. There was no place to hide, nowhere to run. The sailors grew fearful and everyone cried out to their own gods. In desperation, they threw the cargo into the sea to help lighten the load of the ship. But the prophet Jonah had gone down below the deck and fallen into a deep sleep (1:5).

The verb hurled (*tul*) is used four times in this episode (1:4, 5, 12, 15).

- Then the Lord sent (*tul*) a great wind (1:4);
- and they threw (*tul*) the cargo into the sea to lighten the ship (1:5);
- Jonah said, "Pick me up and throw me (*tul*) into the sea" (1:12);
- Then they took Jonah and threw him (*tul*) overboard (1:15).

The Lord's hurling of the wind seems to counter Jonah's defiance. Arnold proposes that the imagery is suggestive of a metaphorical wrestling match between God and Jonah.[5] The rivalry is magnified with the continuing actions of hurling and throwing, culminating in Jonah himself being hurled into the sea.

As the storm grows worse, the sailors panic. They start throwing things out to lighten the ship (1:5b), considering loss of cargo immaterial compared to saving their lives. Their distress and the danger also drives them to invoke help from the deities they are familiar with. These pagan sailors pray desperately, hoping that somehow a divine being out there would rescue them.

---

5. Arnold, *Wrestling with God*, 98.

Jonah, however, is not exerting any religious effort at all. In contrast to the sailors, he is sleeping instead of praying! He has gone down below the deck to sleep. The verb describing Jonah's flight means to "descend" or "go down" (*yarad*) and is frequently repeated, as if to uncover his adamant intent.

- He went down (*yarad*) to Joppa (1:3a).
- He found a ship . . . went aboard (*yarad*) and sailed . . . to flee from the LORD (1:3b).
- Jonah had gone (*yarad*) below deck, where he lay down and fell into a deep sleep (1:5).

This is a picture of Jonah as a fugitive – on the run, "going down" and downward, away from God's destination for him. This movement of Jonah descending and withdrawing may signify his wanting to die, to be relieved of living. His own request to the sailors to throw him into the sea (1:12) may reflect his inner longing to be disposed of completely.[6] Nonetheless, my own view is that Jonah is not yet ready to die or to commit suicide. He appears to hold on to his faith in "the LORD, the God of heaven, who made the sea and the dry land" as he professes to the pagan sailors (1:9). Yet, the whole time Jonah may simply be parroting a creed that he unwilling to live by.

Jonah fell into a deep sleep (*radam*). There are only a few Hebrew verbs that depict "sleeping." The verb *radam* describes the deepest state of sleep. Jonah is resting, whereas the sailors are in a state of restlessness. Jonah is sleeping deeply, whereas the sailors are praying frantically. Jonah is blissfully unaware of the situation, whereas the sailors are trying to find a way out. What a contrast between Jonah and the sailors!

Even when the captain of the ship wakes Jonah and urges him to pray, the prophet remains passive (1:5b–6). Clearly, Jonah understands that this mighty storm is a result of his disobedience, yet he shows no concern for divine judgment or even for his own life.

---

6. Perry, *The Honeymoon Is Over*, 6.

NATURAL CALAMITIES AND PATRON SAINTS

What do people usually do when natural calamities like typhoons, storms, fires, or earthquakes suddenly hit them? Many call out to their own gods or goddesses, and even make personal vows or promises in return for their own safety.

In the Philippine setting, under the religious influence of reverence for the divine being, many devoted believers would pay tribute to their patron saints. Filipinos are fond of celebrating *fiestas* (religious festival) throughout the year in different regions of the country. During these festivities, devoted Filipinos pay tribute to their local patron saint and even pay homage to their *barrio*'s (village's) namesake for granting them good harvest and good health.[1] Many of these festivities are very similar to local folk beliefs and religious rites in nature. Even before the arrival of the Spaniards with their Catholicism, the Filipinos already practiced local pagan worship, like anitism – its original meaning is "ancestral spirit." As in any human culture, the people's urge to cry out to their gods in times of crisis is seen as natural. Upon relief from danger or death, these gods are worshiped and remembered for requests granted or prayers answered.

There is a human tendency to seek a higher being when confronted with impending trouble and death. In Buddhism, the phrase 有求必應 (*you qiu bi ying*) speaks of religion that meets one's needs. Yet our one true God – who is all-knowing, all-powerful, as well as loving – does not always or immediately grant our requests, but responds with "yes," "wait," or even "no" as he, in his wisdom, deems best for us.

---

1. "Philippine Visayan Festivals: Dinagyang," http://www.adelinefilamfood.com/2016/12/19/philippine-visayan-festivals-dinagyang/, posted on December 19, 2016, accessed January 24, 2018.

The sailors, with their expertise and experience, may have sensed that this was an unusual storm. Perhaps they began to wonder if someone in their midst might have caused this storm by displeasing the gods. So they say to one another, "Come, let us cast lots to find out who is responsible for this calamity" (1:7). One way of determining responsibility for a calamity was to cast lots. In the original Hebrew, the word "lots" is in its plural form. These sailors are not content with the outcome from just one lot.[7] Perhaps they were keen to ensure that they did not accuse the wrong person. Interestingly, the lot falls on Jonah. Perhaps on each occasion the lot fell on Jonah! Of course, it is God who makes it happen (Prov 16:33; Acts 1:26).[8] Having singled out Jonah as the person responsible for the stormy sea, the sailors demand answers: "Tell us, who is responsible for making all this trouble for us? What kind of work do you do? Where do you come from? What is your country? From what people are you?" (1:8). The sailors must have been surprised by Jonah's indifference amid the great storm surging around them. Everyone was caught in the fearsome frenzy except Jonah. When the lot fell on Jonah, they needed to find out more about this man.

The most difficult question for Jonah was probably the second one – "What kind of work (*mela'kah*) do you do?" – which contains an unintentional play on words. The word *mela'kah* bears the same root as *mal'ak* ("messenger"). As a prophet, Jonah is a messenger of God. His task is to run errands and be God's mouthpiece wherever he sends him. Jonah should be running *for* God, not running *away* from God!

Finally, Jonah speaks. Like a Sunday school child, who knows a Bible story but is not yet ready to apply the biblical truth being taught, Jonah recites, "I am a Hebrew and I worship the Lord, the God of heaven, who made the sea and the dry land" (1:9). A perfect answer! But is it? There may well be irony in his declaration.[9] Was Jonah serious when he claimed that he worshiped the Lord, the Creator God? If so, why did his actions contradict his supposed reverence toward this Creator God? Jonah is of sound mind when he gives this answer; he does not seem to be joking with the sailors and the captain. Indeed, Jonah has spoken the truth about himself: (a) "I am a Hebrew." Surrounded

---

7. Rosemary Nixon, *The Message of Jonah: Presence in the Storm*, Bible Speaks Today Series, ed. J. A. Motyer (Downers Grove: IVP Academic, 2003), 91.
8. In Chinese *feng shui*, the oracle coins are used as divination. Daniel Tong, *A Biblical Approach to Feng Shui & Divination* (Singapore: Genesis Books, 2006), 87–89.
9. But Carl Bosma interprets Jonah's statements as a positive testimony. Carl J. Bosma, "Jonah 1:9 – An Example of Elenctic Testimony," *Calvin Theological Journal* 48 (2013): 65–90.

by pagans, Jonah boldly announces his own nationality; and (b) "I worship the Lord, the God of heaven, who made the sea and the dry land." He even dares to declare his own faith. But Jonah's life contradicts the profession of his lips, for Jonah also reveals to them the reason he is taking this voyage – to flee from the Lord God. Unspoken questions arise: How could Jonah even think of fleeing from the presence of the Lord? Did he really believe that he could run away from the creator of heaven, sea, and dry land? How could a mere human ever win against a divine being whose ways are beyond human understanding?

In the original language, Jonah's answer to the sailors is: "The Lord, the God of heaven, I fear, who made the sea and dry land" (1:9). The verbless clause brings out his emphasis on this Creator-God.[10] I "fear" (*yare*) the Lord means "revere," implying worship. Such fear should compel Jonah to demonstrate a great respect for his God, quite unlike the fear of those pagan sailors who were merely terrified of God. Jonah knows that the storm is directed by God upon him, but the sailors do not; nor do they know anything of a covenant with the Lord God of creation. Yet Jonah's action of fleeing from God does not match his utterance about fearing the Lord. His running away proves his lack of understanding of who God is and what God could do. Jonah's faith in God is undergoing testing and stretching at this moment. Perhaps he now begins to wonder if God is pursuing him, calling him to go and preach to the city of Nineveh. Yet, he may also feel that because he opposed God, he has ruined his relationship with the Lord.

Jonah's revelation heightens the sailors' fear. The original clause is "the men feared with a great fear" (1:10a). In the Hebrew text, in addition to the adjective extremely or "great," the root "fear" (*yr*) is used twice to add emphasis to the sense of panic.

Scarcely had Jonah given utterance to the shocking truth that he was running away from the Lord when the sailors ask in panic, "What have you done?" (1:10b). This recalls the question God posed to Eve in the garden of Eden: "What is this you have done?" (Gen 3:13). The frightened sailors are expressing moral outrage at what they perceive as unthinkably foolish behavior. They seem to be saying, in effect, "How could you possibly do such a thing?"

The verb "running away" (*baraḥ*) is mentioned twice and "from the Lord" appears three times within the first ten verses of chapter 1. The repetition emphasizes the seriousness of Jonah's actions:

---

10. Youngblood, *Jonah: God's Scandalous Mercy*, 78–79.

- Jonah ran away (*baraḥ*) from the LORD (1:3a)
- After paying the fare . . . to flee (*baraḥ*) from the LORD (1:3b)
- They [the sailors] knew he was running away (*baraḥ*) from the LORD (1:10b)

The phrase "from the LORD" is literally "from the face of the LORD," meaning from his presence. The Lord's "face" signifies his blessing (Exod 33:14). In the OT, the people of God longed to see the face of God and live before his presence (Pss 31:17; 67:2). God hiding his face meant disaster for the people (Deut 31:17; 32:20; Isa 8:17; 54:8). The people of God longed to live before his face – his countenance – receiving his favor.[11] Asians use "face" symbolically to portray either favor or displeasure. "Showing one's face" to another means giving honor to that person; "hiding one's face" depicts shame. In the traditional Chinese imperial court, the emperor would not show his face to his subordinate if he was not happy. In this instance, however, it was not God hiding his face, but Jonah hiding from the Lord. Jonah's fleeing from God's face implies his displeasure with the Lord. The sailors are so "terrified" (1:10a) because they understand the gravity of Jonah's disobedience. How ironic that these pagan sailors were eager to do what was deemed right before the Lord God while God's messenger was running away from him.

Jonah portrays passive-aggressive behavior toward his commission from God. Martel and Cirino say: "People with passive-aggressive behavior express their negative feelings subtly through their actions instead of handling them directly. This creates a separation between what they say and what they do."[12] Jonah opposes God's call to go to Nineveh by his flight to Tarshish – totally the opposite direction from his mission destination. Jonah describes himself as a Hebrew who worships the Creator God, yet his failure to worship this God is seen both in his disobedience and in his failure to call upon the Lord in the storm.

This story demonstrates God's omniscience, omnipotence and omnipresence. The Creator God demonstrates his power over creation in a mighty storm. He knows what Jonah is thinking, where Jonah is hiding and how Jonah is to be saved. Jonah tries to run away from God's presence, but the Lord demonstrates his omnipresence – he is everywhere, and no one can hide from him (Ps 139:7–12).

---

11. See the priestly blessing in Numbers 6:24–26.
12. Janelle Martel and Erica Cirino, "Passive Aggressive Personality," https://www.healthline.com/health/passive-aggressive-personality-disorder, accessed December 1, 2018.

1:11–16 Facing the Consequences of Sin

The sailors' cross-examination of Jonah has not helped the situation. The sea becomes increasingly turbulent and the sailors grow desperate. From inquisitors, their role now shifts to that of a jury trying to decide what penalty to impose on the guilty party. The difference here is that they ask the culprit to recommend his own penalty: "What should we do to you to make the sea calm down for us?" (1:11). Jonah already knows the solution to this stormy situation. "Pick me up and throw me into the sea," he says, "and it will become calm" (1:12). In contrast to the turbulence raging around him, Jonah speaks calmly, as if this solution has no impact at all on his own welfare.

Is Jonah's offer motivated by concern for the welfare of these pagan sailors? Is Jonah being both brave and unselfish in proposing this solution? Jonah knows that he is guilty: "I know that it is my fault that this great storm has come upon you" (1:12). Yet there is no evidence of shame or remorse. If Jonah was indeed prepared to sacrifice himself, why did he not simply throw himself into the sea? Why put the sailors in the dreadful position of having to take such an outrageous step? The reader may wonder if Jonah is simply bluffing. Nevertheless, Jonah seems serious, and quite certain that the storm would cease if he was thrown into the sea (1:12). Is Jonah acting like a rebellious teenager, trying to get even with parents who, he knows, love him deeply? Is Jonah thinking, in adolescent fashion, "Come and get me yourself, God. If you can get those sailors to throw me into the sea, you win and so be it! But it won't be easy for these scared guys to hurl me into the stormy sea." Jonah seems incapable of comprehending the loving kindness of the Lord God. Instead, he wrestles with God like an immature teenager.

Ignoring Jonah's suggestion, the sailors "did their best to row back to land" (1:13), trying to save the lives of everyone aboard, including Jonah. Perhaps they were afraid to lay a hand upon the messenger of God. However, as the sea grew wilder, the sailors decide to follow Jonah's advice. But first they cry out to the Lord God, asking that he would not hold them accountable and that they would not have to die for killing an innocent man (1:14). Reluctantly, the sailors throw Jonah into the sea. Immediately, the raging sea grows calm (1:15). This sudden, almost magical, change in circumstances brings about a change of heart in the sailors. The suddenly quiet sea is a testament of God's approval of their action in throwing Jonah overboard. It appears that the God of heaven, creator of sea and land, is satisfied.

Now the sailors greatly fear God in the sense of worship, acknowledging his presence and power. While this is the second time the narrator emphasizes the fear of the sailors (1:10, 16), it is the first time he mentions that the great fear of the sailors is directed to the Lord God himself. In the earlier instance, the sailors were afraid of Jonah's Creator God and fearful of the danger that threatened them. But now, after throwing Jonah into the sea, their "fear with a great fear" has the Lord as the object of their trust. Now their fear (*yare*) is that of those who worship the Lord. Jonah, despite his creed-like confession (1:9), did not really fear the Lord; but these pagan sailors are now worshiping the Lord. In contrast with Jonah – who claimed to know the Creator God who controlled the sea, yet neglected to call upon him during the storm – the pagan sailors now "offered a sacrifice to the Lord and made vows to him" (1:16).

Every chapter of Jonah has instances of prayer, either by pagan people (1:5; 3:8–9) or by the prophet Jonah (2:1–9; 4:3, 8). Ironically, when the storm rages at sea, it is the pagan sailors who are calling and crying out to their own gods; while Jonah is sound asleep. Even when the captain shakes him awake and urges him to pray, Jonah says nothing. It is only when the sailors draw lots and the lot falls on Jonah that he gives a "testimony" of sorts and speaks of his faith in God. Even then, Jonah does not pray to the Lord, although the pagan sailors cry out to God both before and after throwing Jonah into the sea. Although indirectly and passively, Jonah has testified about the Lord God to the pagans on board the ship, and they now believe in this one true God.

1:17 – 2:10 REPENTANCE OF THE PROPHET

I began writing this chapter from the delivery room, where my daughter Ruth was about to give birth to her firstborn child. Ruth was brought to hospital on a Saturday night because she was experiencing painful contractions; but her water bag had not yet broken. It was Monday by the time our first grandchild, Abigail, was born. The following Saturday, our women's prayer group reflected on Jonah chapter 2. Jonah cries, "the currents swirled about me; all your waves and breakers swept over me . . . seaweed was wrapped around my head" (2:3b, 5b). Just as Abigail, cushioned by the water bag, was kept safe inside her mother's womb, God in his sovereignty directed his creation and orchestrated events to keep Jonah alive inside a large fish.

In the English translations of the Bible, the first chapter of Jonah ends with the words, "Now the Lord provided a huge fish to swallow Jonah, and Jonah was in the belly of the fish three days and three nights" (1:17).[13] But in

---

13. The following versions follow the LXX, the Septuagint, which is the Greek translation of the Hebrew text: kjv, niv, neb, nasv, Living Bible, Good News, and Amplified Bible.

other versions of the Bible, such as the French and German translations, this is the opening verse of the second chapter of Jonah.[14] Thus, in the Hebrew text, Jonah 1:17 is numbered as 2:1 and Jonah 2:1–10 is numbered as 2:2–11.

This commentary favors the Hebrew text, whereby chapter 1 deals with the theme of God's judgment on Jonah and chapter 2 focuses on God's grace. Accordingly, chapter 1 closes with Jonah floundering in the sea, while chapter 2 begins with God preparing a big fish to swallow Jonah and ends with the prophet safely "vomited" onto dry land. This arrangement also makes clearer the structure of the two dialogue patterns between Jonah and God (1:17 – 2:10 and 4:1–11). In the first dialogue, Jonah cries out to God in a prayer of thankful deliverance; in the second, Jonah challenges God with his prayer of sorrowful defiance.

Here is the detailed structure of the first dialogue (1:17 – 2:10):

- A God sends the fish to save Jonah (1:17 – 2:10)
  - B Jonah prays to the Lord inside the fish (2:1–7)
  - B Jonah praises the Lord with a vow inside the fish (2:8–9)
- A God orders the fish to let Jonah go alive (2:10) – Relief for the Prophet

Note the parallel pattern between the first dialogue above (1:17 – 2:10) and the second dialogue below (4:1–11):

- A' God's compassion on Nineveh (4:1–11)
  - B' Jonah prays to the Lord in dismay (4:1–2)
  - B' Jonah pleads with the Lord to let him die (4:3–9)
- A' God expresses his compassion in question form to Jonah (4:10–11) – Reproof from God

The book of Jonah is brief but viewing its structure from an angle which follows the Hebrew text brings to the surface another aspect of its hidden compact design. Jonah 1:17a, 1:17b – 2:9 and 2:10 form a chiastic arrangement, showing the sovereign action of the Creator God in the life of Jonah.

- A The Lord commissions a great fish to swallow up Jonah (1:17a)
  - B Jonah is in the belly of the fish three days and three nights (1:17b)
  - B' Jonah prays to the Lord from the belly of the fish (2:1–9)
- A' The Lord commands the fish to vomit out Jonah (2:10)

---

14. These translations follow the MT – that is, the Hebrew text.

Interestingly, both chapters 1 and 2 end with sacrifices and vows (1:16; 2:9). These two chapters present parallels between Jonah's experience and that of the pagan sailors. Both face a similar crisis and cry to the Lord God, acknowledging his sovereignty; both are physically saved, and offered worship and make vows to God; and both seem to shout out that salvation comes from the Lord! Here are two tables presenting the parallels in these chapters; the first table has Jonah as the primary character, and the second compares the sailors with Jonah.

The Parallels

First: Jonah as the primary character in chapters 1 and 2

	Jonah as the Primary Character	
	Chapter 1	**Chapter 2**
Crisis	Faced with stormy sea (1:4)	Inside the belly of the fish (1:17)
Their Response	Asleep (1:5b–6)	Prayed to the Lord God (2:7)
God's Response	Provided a fish to swallow Jonah (1:17)	Commanded the fish to vomit Jonah (2:10)

Second: The sailors in comparison with Jonah in chapters 1 and 2

	Chapter 1	**Chapter 2**
	Focused on the Sailors	**Focused on Jonah**
Crisis	Faced with stormy sea (1:4–5, 11–13)	Fallen into the depths of the sea (2:2–6)
Their Response	Cried out to the Lord God (1:14)	Cried out to the Lord God (2:2, 7)
God's Response	Calmed the raging sea (1:15b)	Brought him out of the pit (2:6, 10)
Their Response	Praise, sacrifice, vows (1:16)	Praise, sacrifice, vows (2:9)

God has been patient with Jonah, like a father towards his erring son. "The Lord provided a huge fish to swallow Jonah, and Jonah was in the belly of the fish" (1:17). Under God's loving care, there in the belly of the fish, Jonah repents. No longer resigned to death, Jonah now remembers the living God and cries out in a prayerful psalm of petition (2:1–7) and thanksgiving praise (2:8–9); amazingly, Jonah prays as if he were already delivered out of the fish. God's grace is lavished upon us, yet we must never presume on it, always remembering that God is true to his character of holiness, justice, and righteousness. God punishes the disobedient Jonah by having him thrown into the sea, yet he also extends grace, bringing him safely to dry land (2:10), where he will receive a second chance – an opportunity to repent and return to the Lord.

1:17 Rescued by God

"Now the LORD provided a huge fish to swallow Jonah, and Jonah was in the belly of the fish three days and three nights." The Hebrew verb "*manah*" (literally, "send," "appoint," "provide") speaks of God's providence. The big fish, coming at the precise time when Jonah is being hurled overboard, serves as God's instrument of deliverance. It is the Lord God himself who sovereignly sends the fish, just as he had sent the wind to blow harshly (1:4). In contrast to Jonah's disobedience and defiance, a huge fish in the sea promptly obeys the Lord. Even God's created fish follows his command, so why not Jonah?

The narrative is silent about the kind of fish that swallowed Jonah. The Septuagint (the Greek translation of the Old Testament) and the New Testament (Matt 12:40) translate it by the indefinite word *ketos*, "a sea monster." Some older English translations use the word "whale" while modern translations use the more general term "big fish."

IS IT A WHALE OR WHAT?

The denial of Jonah's historicity in the nineteenth and twentieth centuries was due largely to the presence of supernatural elements in the narrative. Foremost among these is the miracle of the big fish. Scholars in the nineteenth century regarded the big fish as a mystical theme which also appeared in the Greek sagas of Hercules and Perseus. Some saw indications of Babylonian mythology in the shared motif of dealing with the dragon of the subterranean ocean. Others suggested that Jonah appeared to the superstitious Ninevites as one of the incarnations of Dagan, a creature part-man and part-fish from an ancient Assyrian religious tradition. Jonah, though, is not to be represented to the Ninevites as a fish-god.

Since the whale is the largest sea animal, it is assumed that this is the kind of fish that swallowed Jonah. Some commentators disagree.

They point out that a whale's gullet is far too narrow to swallow a man. In addition, whales or cetaceans do not exist in the Mediterranean. But other commentators claim that not all whales have the same throat form. They say that there are records of whales that can swallow a man or even engulf objects larger than a horse. In 1891, a whale hunter was reported to have been swallowed by a whale and then recovered, unconscious, the next day, from inside the animal after it was harpooned and cut up. In 1915, it was shown that a whale could even save a drowning man if the person managed to negotiate the whale's air supply tract and reach its great laryngeal pouch.[1]

Scholars also note that the sperm whale (*Phyeter microcephalus* or *catodon*) grows to a considerable size (up to 30 meters) and swallows large prey. One such sperm whale, only 14.5 meters long, was caught near the Azores (one of the two autonomous regions of Portugal), and contained a perfectly preserved living squid, 10 meters long, in its stomach. Killer whales or orcas, 6 to 10 meters long, also swallow large prey like dolphins, narwhals, sea bass, and seals.[2] These mammals are said to have been present in the Mediterranean during the Middle Ages.

Other commentators suggest that the big fish in Jonah could be a certain species of shark. Entire human bodies have been found in one type of shark, *Lamia canis carcharis*. There are recent examples of people having been recovered alive from them. In 1758, a sailor who fell into the sea was swallowed by a shark, then spat back out after the ship captain shot a harpoon at the shark. Based on the captain's testimony, the sailor toured Europe and exhibited the shark.[3]

These stories of fish swallowing people are not to be dismissed as ridiculous. But one serious difficulty remains in the Jonah narrative: Whereas modern sailors allegedly swallowed by large sea animals were recovered unconscious, wounded, or dead, the prophet Jonah was very much alive, and fully conscious both mentally and emotionally. He was even able to compose a psalm of penitent prayer and thanksgiving praise before being vomited out by the fish!

---

1. Rosa S. Ching, "An Analytical Key and Exegetical Commentary on the Book of Jonah," (Master's thesis, Biblical Seminary of the Philippines, 1980), 39–40.
2. Arnold, *Wrestling with God*, 79.
3. Arnold, 80.

The text does not speak of a whale but of a "great fish" (1:17; 2:1, 10). Nevertheless, Jonah being swallowed by a great fish and spewed out alive three days later is without parallel in known human history. Much has been written concerning the great fish. From the early Christian period, there have been different views surrounding the nature of this book. Some scholars, such as Origen (AD 185–254), favored an allegorical approach; others, such as Augustine (AD 354–430), preferred a more literal one. Nevertheless, both approaches are grounded in a profound reverence for sacred Scripture as the word of God.[15] This big fish is especially "provided" or appointed or designated (1:17) by God the creator for this specific task of saving Jonah.

Consider the action verb "provided." It is best translated "appointed" or "sent," and is used four times in the book – with Jonah as the recipient of God's providing or appointing:

- God provided (*manah*) a fish (1:17);
- God provided (*manah*) a vine (4:6);
- God provided (*manah*) a worm (4:7);
- God provided (*manah*) a scorching wind (4:8).

The action verb depicts God's intervention on behalf of the prophet. Jonah affirms God as the creator and God demonstrates that he is indeed in control. Although God could have left Jonah to the mercies of the sea, he did not. Instead, he saves Jonah from the raging storm.

The second part of this verse is intriguing: "and Jonah was in the belly of the fish three days and three nights" (1:17b). The phrase is an expression of a long period of time. The precise time is echoed when Jesus makes reference to Jonah's story to indicate the time he would spend in the tomb: "three days and three nights" (Matt 12:40). It is also significant that Jesus speaks of "the sign of the prophet Jonah" (or "the sign of Jonah") three times in the Gospels (Matt 12:38–41; 16:4; Luke 11:29–32), on each occasion in the context of unbelief. The period of time could also be the length of time it would take for the fish and the wind to cast Jonah on the banks of his homeland. It is also possible that God, in his sovereignty, might even have ordered the fish to "vomit" Jonah out at a suitable location, near the road to Nineveh.

The relationship of Jonah to Christ can be seen in two aspects of Jesus's ministry: first, his passion, death and resurrection; second, God's universal grace and compassion for all humankind. Jesus and Jonah come from the same geographical area, for Gath-Hepher is located only five kilometers northeast

---

15. Nixon, *The Message of Jonah*, 130.

of Nazareth. The Pharisees during Jesus's time forgot or ignored this fact when they rebuked Nicodemus for defending Jesus: "you will find that a prophet does not come out of Galilee" (John 7:52). Each time Jesus refers to the "sign" of Jonah, it is in the context of the doubting Pharisees or crowds demanding miraculous signs from Jesus. The "sign of Jonah," together with the "three days and three nights," points to two miracles: Jonah inside the belly of the fish and the mass conversion of the Ninevites after Jonah's proclamation.

Some commentators draw attention to the contrasts between Jonah and Jesus. Jonah was imprisoned inside the fish as a punishment for his disobedience, but Jesus was always perfectly submissive to the Father. When Jonah obeyed God and proclaimed his message, there was mass repentance among the Ninevites, but Jesus's ministry, and even his death and resurrection, yielded little fruit among the Jews, particularly the Pharisees and other religious leaders.

Other commentators see messianic typology in Jonah, and Jesus's reference to the "sign of Jonah" underlines the correspondence between Jonah's story and that of Jesus.

Suffering: First, both Jonah and Jesus struggle to accept the will of God. Jonah flees to Tarshish in opposition to God; Jesus, however, endures great physical, emotional, and spiritual distress in the garden of Gethsemane: "And being in anguish, he prayed more earnestly, and his sweat was like drops of blood falling to the ground" (Luke 22:44). Second, there is deliverance from death: Jonah repents, and God allows him to live; Jesus is resurrected, for death could not imprison the holy one of God.

Salvation and second chances: Both Jonah and Jesus are called to urgently proclaim God's salvation; their ministry centers on preaching repentance and offering second chances. Jonah proclaims, "Forty more days and Nineveh will be overthrown" (3:4b), offering the Ninevites a chance to repent or otherwise face destruction. Jesus begins his public ministry with the call, "Repent, for the kingdom of heaven has come near" (Matt 4:17). Jonah, whose name means "dove," is sent to the Ninevites for their mass conversion. The Holy Spirit descends upon Jesus in the form of a dove at his baptism, which marks the beginning of his public ministry (Matt 3:16; Mark 1:10; Luke 3:22; John 1:32).

Truly, our Lord Jesus regarded the miracle of the fish, the period of Jonah's stay inside the fish, and the repentance of the Ninevites as actual events. This attitude of Jesus regarding the historicity of Jonah's narrative is authoritative support for its authenticity.

2:1–9 Remembrance of God

While the narrative portion of book of Jonah describes the actions of Jonah and their consequences, the poetry in this section gives voice to Jonah's inner feelings. Almost the entirety of chapter 2 is a prayer of thanksgiving that demonstrates Jonah's trust in God. It begins with petition and closes with praise. This is the only poetic passage in the book of Jonah. A Chinese quote says 麻雀雖小, 五臟俱全 (*ma que sui xiao, wu zang ju quan* – "The sparrow may be small, but all its vital organs are there"). Although relatively short, the book of Jonah is complete in every detail, and includes both prose and poetry.

Poetry is a medium conducive to expressing one's emotions to the fullest. In my high school days, I never did well with prose compositions, but I won many prizes in poetry contests. In composing poetry, I found myself able to express my emotions unreservedly. Poetry is normally composed from the heart, as it expresses the feelings of the poet. Poetry also speaks to us in times of crisis when we feel overwhelmed.[16] Chinese poems are often gloomy and pessimistic.

---

16. Villanueva, *Lamentations*, 34.

SINGING OUT IN TROUBLED TIMES

Many poetic prayers of petition to God have been composed by people undergoing various kinds of trials. These may later be set to music and be used as songs of praise and thanksgiving. Here is an original Filipino composition, a crying to the Lord in a time of trouble.

Song in Tagalog Language:	English Translation by Rosa C. Shao:
Nasaan Kaya Ako Papuri Singers[1]	**Where Would I Be** Praise Singers
Naglalaro sa hangin ang buhay ko 'Di malaman kung sa'n ang tungo Sumasabay sa agos ng mundong ito Ako'y gulung-gulo	My life is tossed Along with the wind Where it's going No one even knows Going with the flow of this hurried life I'm in frenzied turmoil
'Di ko na malaman kung ano ang gagawin sa buhay ko Pawang kalungkutan, walang pagbabago Kapaguran ang laging nadarama ko	I do not even know what to do with my life anymore All sadness, nothing new Exhaustion only is what I'm feeling
Kabiguan ang naging dahilan Naghahanap ng liwanag Layaw ng laman Sya'ng pansamantalang kasagutan sa aking hanap	Frustration the cause even as I look for light Desire of the flesh Just a temporary answer to my quest
Chorus: Nasaan kaya ako Hesus, kung wala Ka 'Di ko na malaman kung sa'n ako pupunta Maaaring nasa hangin pa ako 'Di alam kung saan ang tungo	Chorus: Where would I be Jesus, if not For You I would not have known where I'm going Maybe I'd still live in the wind not knowing where to go

---

1. Permission has been secured from Papuri for the song, "Nasaan Kaya Ako" sung by Papuri Singers, https://www.youtube.com/watch?v=48s9bfGMIPc, accessed July 12, 2018.

2:1–7 Praying to God

Jonah models how we should pray in times of crisis, highlighting the importance of thankfulness and praise even *before* our prayers are answered. Jonah may well have confessed and repented while lying in the belly of the big fish, but the text is silent about any actual words of penitence.

From inside the belly of the big fish, Jonah bares his heart to God (2:1). This brief narration is followed by Jonah's poetic prayer. Surrounded by devastating darkness, feeling doomed, Jonah turns to the Lord God in prayer. In a poetic monologue – an intense and emotional outpouring, expressed in a plethora of powerful images – Jonah recounts how he was brought back from the brink of death.

> In my distress I called to the LORD,
>   and he answered me.
> From deep in the realm of dead I called for help,
>   and you listened to my cry. (2:2)

Although Jonah starts out by referring to God in the third person, almost immediately he switches to the first person, pouring out his distress directly to God and praying confidently for God's deliverance. We see an "I-Thou" relationship between Jonah and the Lord, strikingly similar to Psalms 18:6 and 120:1.

In 2:2a, Jonah is speaking *about* the Lord. But in 2:2b, he is speaking *to* the Lord. The former is a testimony about his whole experience whereas the latter is a direct address to the Lord about his predicament.

Jonah knows that it is God who is behind all this: "You hurled me into the depths, into the very heart of the seas" (2:3a). Perhaps he also recognizes that the task God assigned to him is not complete yet. The Creator God demonstrates his mighty power not only in appointing a fish but also in taking charge of Jonah's life. Jonah 2:3b, "and the currents swirled about me; all your waves and breakers swept over me," may add to the imagery of the wrestling match between God and Jonah. But Jonah is now submissive, willing to loosen his grip and let God be the God who saves. Even as currents swirl around him and waves crash over him, Jonah trusts in God's deliverance: "yet I will look again toward your holy temple" (2:4b). The images of swirling currents and seaweed wrapped around his head are recalling a baby inside her mother's water bag with the umbilical cord around her.

One can imagine the smelly and slimy waters inside the fish, threatening to suffocate Jonah. Yet Jonah continues to pray, clinging to his faith in God even as he describes in poetic terms his distressing near-death experience and the feeling of being "banished" from God's sight (2:4a). For the people of God, God's "sight" (literally, "eyes") expresses his care and concern (Deut 11:12; Jer 24:6), as well as his love and guidance (Pss 32:8; 33:18). Interestingly, "sight" is also an Asian expression, conveying how a teacher cares for the success of his students or how a mother cherishes her daughter. Despite feeling banished Jonah holds on to hope, affirming, "I will look again toward your holy temple" (2:4b). Even when he is threatened by "the engulfing waters" (2:5a) and feels his life "ebbing away" (2:7a), Jonah "remembers" (2:7a) God with faith and hope. This confidence is echoed by David:

> But I, by your great love,
> can come into your house,
> in reverence I bow down
> toward your holy temple. (Ps 5:7)

Another description of the peril of death heightens the magnitude of God's salvation. The grim situation of being inside the belly of the fish three days and three nights is akin to being buried alive. Jonah pictures himself with seaweed wrapped around him: "the engulfing waters threatened me, the deep surrounded me; seaweed was wrapped around my head" (2:5).

Inside the fish's belly, Jonah cries out to God unceasingly, persisting in his faith that God will deliver him. The phrase "I sank down" (*yarad*) is a reminder of his earlier rebelliousness; and this is the fourth time the verb is used in the book of Jonah (see 1:3, 5b). The phrase also expresses his feeling of separation from the Lord. He finds himself sinking down to the roots of the mountains with the bars of earth shut behind him and his life ebbing away. "But you, LORD my God, brought my life up from the pit" (2:6b). Jonah's hope is that the Lord God himself will bring him up from the pit. The word "pit" is synonymous with "grave," signifying the place of death (Isa 38:17; 51:14; Ezek 28:8). This prayer is similar to David's thanksgiving psalm:

> Praise the LORD, my soul . . .
> who redeems your life from the pit . . ." (Ps 103:1a, 4a)

In the midst of his fear and suffering, Jonah calls on the Lord to take control of his life. Jonah would not succumb to death without thinking of God, the only help he could count on (Pss 18:4–6; 69:1–3). Twice he mentions God's holy temple (2:4, 7). To a worshiping Jew the temple signified God's presence. In Solomon's prayer of dedication of the temple, he affirmed that God hears from heaven and acts (1 Kgs 8:32, 34, 36). Jonah knows his prayer book; he is familiar with these psalms and prayers that help him cry out with faithful confidence. As he cries out for God's help, he senses the intensification of the dreadful and deadly situation in which he finds himself. But as he continues to cry out to God, his thoughts shift and his prayer becomes an expression of gratitude for God's sure salvation.

We reflected on this passage in my Bible study group. Like Jonah inside the belly of the fish, we need to be able to pray to God and even praise our Lord in troubled times as well as in good times. The hostess confessed that she had been angry with God for three years because her fifty-seven-year-old mother had passed away suddenly, leaving her father a widower. Although she had been a believer for years, she would not talk to God because she could not see his goodness in allowing this sorrow in her family. Yet God had been patient with her. Subsequently, her father remarried, and she joyfully welcomed her stepmother into the family. She finally accepted that life is filled with both joy and sorrow, just as the sky may be sunny, cloudy, rainy, or even stormy. God is sovereign, mighty in power, yet also gentle, sympathetic, and patient with us.

The woman seated next to the hostess was touched by the word, "I *remembered* you, LORD" (2:7a, italics mine). She shared that many times, when we encounter difficulties in life, we tend to seek human help and forget to turn first to God. We must remember that our Lord God is near to us and that he should be our first recourse and not our last resort. My husband once wisely admonished, "We should not blame God in bad situations, and we should never run away from God even when tragedy hits home. Because when everything and everyone else fails us, God alone is there for us, no other but God! He is all we have, so why leave God out of our lives?" Jonah teaches us to cling to God's faithfulness, remembering God's character of goodness, greatness, and gentleness in dealing with our human frailty, foolishness, and forgetfulness, and persevering in praying to God and pondering before his holy temple – that is, his presence wherever we are.

2:8–9 Praising God

This next part of Jonah's poetic prayer proclaims the truth about worshiping worthless idols. How pitiful that "those who cling to worthless idols turn away from God's love for them" (2:8). Jonah is ready to proclaim God's steadfast love even while inside the belly of the fish. He uses a negative statement to express the positive blessings in worshiping God.

This may call to mind how the pagan sailors started calling out to their gods when the storm at sea threatened their lives. Each one called upon their gods but to no avail. It was useless to worship false idols. Then Jonah introduced them to the Lord, the God of heaven whom he worshiped. These pagan sailors witnessed how the raging sea calmed down at once when they threw Jonah overboard just as he had instructed.

Jonah ends his prayer of thanksgiving with grateful praise. He even binds himself with a vow, saying:

> But I, with shouts of grateful praise,
> will sacrifice to you.
> What I have vowed I will make good.
> I will say, "Salvation comes from the Lord." (2:9)

Jonah does not specify the kind of sacrifice he has vowed to make; but we can speculate that it would include fulfilling his mission to go to Nineveh, which he later does (3:3). Jonah is still inside the fish, perhaps barely alive, yet he is both joyful and grateful as he shouts praises to the Lord his God. He literally shouts out, "Only God can give salvation," with such confidence, as if he was already safe and sound. If we understand that our God is not only great but also good and gentle, then we would include thanksgiving praise in every prayer request we utter, thanking God even before our prayers are answered. "Gratitude makes sense of our past, brings peace for today, and creates vision for tomorrow."[17]

Nick Vujicic, who was born without limbs, echoed such praise to God. Even in a Christian home, it had not been easy for him growing up with such deformities. He testified that, as a young boy, he once contemplated suicide. But God pulled him through so that he could be God's useful servant. Now he goes around the world telling people that if we invite God to forgive our sins each day and each night, we will grow in faith and in favor; God will perfect his work in us and that is what is meant by "good."[18] What may seem a burden to us could become a blessing according to God's purpose when we come into a right relationship with God.

After listening to our study on Jonah's prayer of thanksgiving praise, two other ladies in our Bible study group shared these enriching spiritual lessons. One said that when times of distress threaten to sweep us away, we instinctively try to swim upstream, against the current, not even pondering what God

---

17. Melody Beattie, https://www.brainyquote.com/quotes/melody_beattie_134462, accessed February 16, 2018.
18. Nicolas James Vujicic, *Be the Hands and Feet: Living Out God's Love for All His Children* (Colorado Springs, CO: WaterBrook, 2018), 81.

could be telling us through the situation we are in. And so we may miss out on what God wants us to learn during such a time of crisis. Her friend beside her marveled at how Jonah was able to pray, and even thank God, in the midst of chaotic waters when he was in danger of drowning. Jonah shows us how to maintain an unswerving faith in God through life's difficult ordeals. Indeed, "the greatest test of faith is when you don't get what you want, but still you are able to say, Thank You Lord."[19]

2:10 Relief for the Prophet

Following Jonah's sincere prayer of commitment, the scene shifts from the belly of the fish to dry land: "the LORD commanded the fish, and it vomited Jonah onto dry land" (2:10). In the book of Leviticus, "vomit" was related to the process of cleansing the land due to the pollution of sin (Lev 18:25, 28; 20:22). If the verb in Jonah were in its basic form, it would mean that the fish vomited Jonah because of his hypocrisy. But the verb here is causative – it is God who commanded the fish to vomit Jonah.[20] The action of God in causing the fish to vomit the prophet gives Jonah a new lease of life to fulfill his mission.

The next step is to get Jonah to Nineveh. The fish vomits Jonah onto dry land, but the text is silent as to the specific location. Perhaps it is a place near Jonah's original port of embarkation or somewhere on the road to Nineveh. The fish responded instantly to God's command. Now it is Jonah's turn to promptly fulfill the vow he had made while inside the belly of the fish. Earlier, he responded to God with a silent "no"; this time, will he say "yes"?

Psalms to Calm One's Trauma

Music is a universal language. Every era of human history has its own musical forms and norms. Many hymns, choruses, and anthems express and extol the varied human experiences, both good and bad. Music – in songs, poems, and even plays – helps people to process dramatic and traumatic events in their lives. Composing, singing, and listening to hymns and songs may help people make sense of difficult events or situations and even cope with things which don't make sense.

A near-drowning, followed by three days and three nights inside the belly of the fish, would certainly count as a life-threatening, not to mention distressing and disturbing, experience! Composing a psalm may have helped Jonah to process his pain and perplexity. It is interesting that many of Jonah's

---

19. A well-known quote from John Hagee.
20. Brent A. Strawn, "On Vomiting: Leviticus, Jonah, Ea(a)rth," *CBQ* 74 (2012): 444–445.

prayerful utterances echo verses from the book of Psalms. Scripture has been, and continues to be, a powerful source of inspiration for hymn and songwriters.

The PSALM method was developed to equip churches to be places of restoration for people who have experienced various kinds of trauma. It aims to bring healing and restore hope to hurting and suffering people. The acronym PSALM is based on Psalm 23, and this is combined with lessons from trauma competency.[21]

Presence: The presence of God is very real in the life of David (and also of Jonah).

Security: The rod and staff are like secure boundaries for God's children.

Affirmation: God's anointing oil is an affirmation of the role for which he has created us.

Listening: Listening, along with observing, helps to understand what is going on inside a person.

Motivation: God's goodness and mercy can heal and minister to even the worst illness or pain.

---

21. Jordan Belser, "The Traumatized Child: Implications for the Church in the Story of Mephibosheth," *JAM* 19, no. 1 (2018): 85–92.

JONAH 3:1 – 4:11
THE SECOND COMMISSION FROM GOD

Despite all our technological advances, we live with so much uncertainty and unpredictability, perhaps more so than in any other period of human history. Our world grows increasingly chaotic and confusing, and not just in the Majority World. Global economic crises affect everyone everywhere, whether rich or poor. Science exerts every effort to eradicate diseases, distance, and discomfort, yet no amount of digital innovation or sophisticated technical tools could ever equip humankind to resolve the problem of evil. Why would Jonah run away from the opportunity to preach against an evil city?

The world today is full of atrocities, not just far away but closer home. Some time ago, Tom, president of an evangelical seminary in the Philippines, received the sad news that his brother had been gunned down by a member of an extremist group. He found comfort in Jesus's words: "I have told you these things, so that in me you may have peace. In this world you will have trouble. But take heart! I have overcome the world" (John 16:33). The bereaved family received the news that the police had arrested the culprit and that he was now in jail. A few weeks later, Tom visited the prison and shared the gospel with his brother's killer. He continued his visits until, one day, the killer became a believer in the Lord Jesus Christ. "Why did you bother to reach out to me after what I did to your brother" asked this new believer. Tom replied: "It was very hard for me to visit you, week after week, knowing you had killed my brother. But the Lord Jesus reminded me that my brother is now in heaven, enjoying eternal life. The love of Christ helped me see that you needed Jesus so badly." The Ninevites were enemies of Israel and had committed many atrocities against them. Just as it was difficult for Tom to share the good news with the man who had hurt him, it was hard for Jonah to share a message of mercy with the people of Nineveh.

The introductory section of this commentary outlined a concentric or chiasmic structure for the book of Jonah. Below is an alternative way of structuring the book, by considering its two parallel sections: chapters 1 – 2 and chapters 3 – 4.[1]

---

1. Adapted from Xian Zhang Wu, *You Don't Know My Heart: Commentary on the Book of Jonah* (Taipei, Taiwan: Taosheng Publishing House of Taiwan Lutheran Church, 2013), 168.

Chapters 1 – 2	Chapters 3 – 4
The word of the Lord to Jonah the first time (1:1–2)	The word of the Lord to Jonah the second time (3:1–2)
Jonah's response (1:3)	Jonah's response (3:3–4)
The pagans' response (1:4–5)	The pagans' response (3:5)
The captain's response (1:6)	The Ninevite king's response (3:6–9)
Interaction between sailors and Jonah (1:7–15a)	Interaction between Ninevites and God (3:10a)
Calamity ceased (1:15b)	Calamity prevented (3:10b)
The sailors' response (1:16)	Jonah's response (4:1)
Jonah with God (1:17 – 2:9)	Jonah with God (4:2–5)
God's response (2:10)	God's response (4:6–11)

In these two sections, Jonah's destinations are the farthest ends of the then known world. The first is a journey of disobedience, heading west, across the sea, and resulting in a failed mission; the second is a journey of obedience, heading east, across land, concluding in a mission accomplished.

This commentary considers this second journey in four main sections: first, the recommissioning of the prophet by God (3:1–4); second, the repentance of the Ninevites, with the whole city – kings, nobles, subjects, and even animals – fasting and covering themselves with sackcloth in humble repentance (3:5–9); third, a consideration of how, when Nineveh repents, God relents and refrains from punishing them (3:10). If the story ended at this point, Jonah would have appeared a hero or superstar. But God has not finished with his messenger yet. The final section of the book (4:1–11) demonstrates that God is more concerned with his servant's character than with the results of his service.

3:1–4 RECOMMISSIONING FROM GOD

Chapter 3 of the book of Jonah places the prophet in the great city of Nineveh. God offers Jonah another chance (3:1–2); and this time, the prophet chooses to obey, going exactly where God sends him and faithfully proclaiming the message entrusted to him (3:3–4).

Jonah 3:1 – 4:11

3:1–2 Recommissioning of the Prophet

The first time God commissioned him, Jonah ran away. Now God recommissions the prophet, offering him another chance. This is both a privilege and a blessing, for not everyone gets a second chance to redeem their past. The Lord God shows his steadfast love to Jonah. A second time he says, "Go to the great city of Nineveh and proclaim to it the message I give you" (3:2). God's commission remains unchanged: it is the same destination and the same task as before. Jonah is the only prophet who is entrusted with the same mission twice. God could easily have chosen another prophet to send to Nineveh; instead, he graciously offers Jonah a second chance, an opportunity to make amends for his disobedience and to do things right.

The second call of the Lord differs from the first in four ways. First, there is no mention of Jonah being "the son of Amittai" (1:1). But there was no necessity to repeat this, since this identification has already been made. In Old Testament narratives, the paternal origin of a person is not usually repeated.

Second, the tone of the recommissioning seems different and there is now a new motivation for the proclamation. In the first call, Jonah was to speak "against" (*'al*) Nineveh because its wickedness had come up before God (1:2). The preposition "against (*'al*) indicates the serious, even threatening, nature of the preaching. In the second call, "Go to the great city of Nineveh and proclaim to it the message I give you" (3:2) the preposition used is "to" (*'el*), which merely indicates that Nineveh is the object and recipient of Jonah's message. To cry out "preach against" Nineveh clearly emphasizes judgment. But to "proclaim to it" is a call to repentance. God's merciful grace is available for the people of Nineveh – if only they are ready to repent of their evil ways.

Third, "proclaim the message that I am giving you" can be translated literally as "proclaim the proclamation that I am speaking to you." The proclamation message comes from the Lord who appoints Jonah to do the task. As a prophet, his proclamation comes directly from the Lord. He is only a messenger who carries the message of the Lord to the people of Nineveh. The Hebrew sentence structure is a play on words, with an imperative verb "proclaim" (*qera*) followed with the noun "proclamation" (*qeri'ah*). It emphasizes the kerygma message of this proclamation coming from the Lord himself to the city of Nineveh and Jonah has to proclaim it accordingly. The additional phrase, "the message I give you" (3:2), is not found in the first calling. This may also be translated "the proclamation that I am speaking to you." The first time, Jonah does not wait for God to spell out what he would have him tell the city of Nineveh and simply takes off grudgingly. The wickedness of the people of Nineveh was so great that Jonah knew about it simply by reputation. The second time around, God speaks like a parent advising a rebellious son who has now come to his senses and returns home to his father. He says to Jonah, "You are to proclaim to her the proclamation that I am speaking to you." The phrase "I am speaking to you" is in the participial tense, specifying the ongoing and continuous message that the prophet was to bring to Nineveh. The emphasis here is that Jonah must only preach the message that God would give him and not any message of his own conception. It is the divine authority behind it that makes this message both vital and valuable.

THE GOD OF SECOND CHANCES

Having received a second chance to serve the Lord, Jonah was able to accomplish his original mission, which was to preach God's message to the city of Nineveh. The Bible tells us about other people who were given the privilege of a second chance to be used by the Lord. Samson (Judg 16), David (2 Sam 12), Peter (John 21), and Mark (Acts 15:36–41; 2 Tim 4:11) were given another chance to rise from where they had fallen. Many of those who given second chances were able to redeem their failures; but there were others who wasted these opportunities. One such person was Balaam, a mercenary, double-minded prophet who practiced divination, and wasted three opportunities to speak as God directed (Num 22:5–7, 10–19, 21–35; 23:12; 31:14 – 16; 2 Pet 2:15–16).

A person who is given a second chance, or multiple chances, is not only privileged, but bears the responsibility to be obedient and to make the most of the new opportunity. The second chance should lead the person to become better, not worse; to let go of the old so that the new may begin.

There are many heartwarming stories of God giving someone another chance to live for him and the person turning his or her life around. One such story is the powerful transformation in the life of Mark Wang, a Chinese immigrant living in the Philippines. In 2005, Mark Wang killed a man while on a drinking spree; and in 2008, he was incarcerated at the Manila City Jail. By God's merciful grace, some local Chinese-Filipino pastors, who were involved in prison ministry, shared the gospel with him. About three years later, having been part of a Bible study group in prison, Mark Wang became a true believer in Jesus Christ. Today, he testifies that the word of God transformed him from the inside out. Now

> Mark preaches in prison, urging others to turn to Jesus Christ and find true joy and peace as well as freedom from all vices and depravities.
>
> Real-life miracles, where people come under the transforming power of Christ's saving grace, are true testaments of renewed life – actually, a second life. In his book, *Catching Your Second Wind to Finish Well*,[1] Carl Richardson speaks about treasuring one's second chances. Consider whether you, like Jonah, have been given a second chance to serve God. How gratefully have you received this privilege? How faithfully are you responding to this opportunity?
>
> ---
>
> 1. Carl H. Richardson, *Catching Your Second Wind to Finish Well* (Tampa, FL: Beyond Borders, 2011).

3:3–4 Response of the Prophet

At least on the surface, it appears that Jonah is obedient to God, for we read that he "obeyed the word of the LORD and went to Nineveh" (3:3a). Now Nineveh was such a large city that it took three days to go through it. Jonah begins his mission by going a day's journey into the city and proclaiming, "Forty more days and Nineveh will be overthrown" (3:4). Jonah's flight to Tarshish "to flee from the LORD" (1:3) and his journey to Nineveh (3:3) are antithetical, showing complete disobedience on the one hand and absolute obedience on the other. Jonah's "yes," however, turns out to be superficial. The next chapter reveals that he is not fully committed to this mission that would eventually save the Ninevites from divine judgment (4:1–3).

The narrative employs two ways to portray the city of Nineveh. First, it describes Nineveh in terms of how God views this city and its people. Second, it narrates that a walk through the city will require three days. Some commentators interpret this to refer to the diameter, going straight through the city; others regard this as the distance around the city (the perimeter or circumference). God refers to Nineveh as a "great city" (1:2; 3:2; 4:11). In the Hebrew, the phrase "an exceedingly great city" (*yir gedolah lelohim*) is literally "a city great to God" – that is, "significant before God" or "worthy before God." Indeed, the narrator also describes Nineveh as a "large city" (3:3). The city is so significant to God that he sent Jonah to preach to its people in order to avert its destruction.

Specifying that "it took three days to go through it" (3:3b) is one way of depicting Nineveh as a massive city. This "three days" resonates with the "three days and three nights" of Jonah's stay inside the belly of the fish (1:17). The name "Nineveh" means "the house of the fishes."[2] And so Jonah is now in a different house of fishes! He enters Nineveh going "a day's journey into the city" or "the walk of a day." It is absurd to assume that Jonah goes through the entire length of the city in a straight line; this is improbable. The three-days' march lends itself to various interpretations. It is possible that the three days refer to the day of arrival, the day to attend to business, and then the day of departure. But taken this way, it is hard to connect "three days" to the size of the city. Assyrian records from Jonah's time point out that the term "Nineveh" could refer either to the city or the province that it governed.[3] Others make reference to the "Assyrian triangle," a region defined by the three cities lying between 15 and 40 kilometers apart (Korsabad, Nineveh, and Nimrod) in a compact group, thus, referring to Nineveh as an entire district.[4]

The description of Nineveh as being a three-day walk (3:3) is also an indicator of the area of Jonah's responsibility. It seems that Jonah does not preach immediately upon entering the city but only after a day's journey, having gone some distance into the city. In fact, Jonah has no need to walk through the entire city because all the Ninevites, "from the greatest to the least" (3:5), repent as soon as the message of God spreads through the city.

What a powerful message coming from the Lord God in just five Hebrew words: "Forty more days and Nineveh will be overthrown" (3:4; compare Gen 19:21, 25, 29; Amos 4:11; Lam 4:9). Although it is possible that Jonah spoke more than these five words, the narrative records just this five-word message. Jonah announces that the city shall be "overthrown" (*hapak*), literally "overturned," "destroyed," or "demolished" from its very foundations. The forty-day time frame in Jonah's proclamation likely echoes the symbolism of a forty-day period in two episodes from the Pentateuch: the flood narrative (Gen 6–9) and Moses's intercession for the Israelites after their sin with the golden calf (Exod 34:28; Deut 9:25). For Jewish readers, these episodes would have served as a warning of God's judgment, now directed toward Nineveh's immoral and evil state. The verb "overthrown" could evoke the story of the destruction of Sodom and Gomorrah, where the same verb is used thrice (Gen 19:21, 25, 29).

---

2. The interpretation of Donald Wisemen cited in Arnold, *Wrestling with God*, 125.
3. John H. Walton, "Jonah," in *Zondervan Illustrated Bible Backgrounds Commentary*, vol. 3, ed. John H. Walton (Grand Rapids: Zondervan, 2009), 113.
4. Arnold, *Wrestling with God*, 126.

On the other hand, the verb "overthrown" also carries the meaning "to change," "to reform," or "to alter" (Exod 14:5; Lev 13:25). This opens up the possibility of an alternative interpretation: "Forty days until Nineveh is reformed." There is, therefore, a sense of ambiguity in Jonah's proclamation. It can be understood as an ultimatum, either for the city's destruction or for its change of heart – that is, repentance by the Ninevites. Jonah was obviously aware of this double message in his proclamation. Despite his own feelings of animosity towards the Ninevites, Jonah proclaimed the message of salvation to Nineveh. His understanding of God as "a gracious and compassionate God, slow to anger and abounding in love" (4:2) is what makes it difficult for Jonah to fully or enthusiastically embrace his mission. Nineveh shall be destroyed if it does not repent and it shall be saved only if it truly repents. Forty days is the deadline given for the great city of Nineveh to repent, reform, and be transformed.

Jonah's job, as God's messenger, is to proclaim God's message of salvation to the city of Nineveh, but also to predict its impending destruction if the people fail to repent. A prophet's role includes both forthtelling and foretelling. To forthtell is to speak a message from God for the designated hour to a designated audience – in this instance, a warning that calls for a conversion of heart. To foretell is to predict something that will take place in the future. Jonah does both. He proclaims God's salvation to Nineveh and also predicts the outcome of that message, an outcome that is dependent on how the Ninevites choose to receive and respond to God's message. The following chart illustrates the difference between forthtelling and foretelling:[5]

Forthtelling	**Foretelling**
To tell forth; to proclaim boldly	To predict; to tell the future before it occurs; to prophesy
Prophets and preachers who speak forth the will and the counsel of God in timely fashion according to the need of the hour	Prophets who, by God's initiative, foretell imminent events

---

5. Paul LeeTan, "What Is the Difference between 'Fore-telling' and 'Forth-telling'?" http://www.tanbible.com/tol_faq/faq_general_02.htm, accessed April 11, 2018.

3:5–9 REPENTING OF THE NINEVITES

Jonah obediently carries out his task, proclaiming the five-word message that God wants him to bring to Nineveh. These five words are all it takes to turn Nineveh upside down, bringing them to humble repentance before God.

3:5–6 Response of the Ninevites

When Jonah preached, the Ninevites believed God and responded with true repentance. The verb "believed" means to be firm, sure, or true. All of them, from the greatest to the least, responded by fasting and putting on sackcloth (3:5). Fasting relates to an inward manifestation of remorse, whereas putting on sackcloth is an outward expression of sadness. Both were signs of repentance (Joel 1:13–14). The king himself heeds Jonah's warning and repents. Four action verbs illustrate the seriousness of the king: "he *rose* from his throne, *took off* his royal robes, *covered himself* with sackcloth and *sat down* in the dust" (3:6, italics added). This demonstrates an attitude of penitence and deep mourning (compare 1 Kgs 21:27). The sincere fast, remorseful actions, and contrite hearts exemplify the kind of faith that pleases God. The faith expressed here is comparable to Abraham's faith in God prior to the covenant of circumcision (Gen 15:6). The verb "believed" (*'mn*) implies full trust in God (3:5).[6]

The Lord God demonstrates that he shows no partiality when he regards the prayers of these Gentile Ninevites as holy and acceptable in his sight. This notion of God showing no partiality is echoed by the apostle Peter after his encounter with the Gentile centurion Cornelius: "I now realize how true it is that God does not show favoritism but accepts from every nation the one who fears him and does what is right" (Acts 10:34–35). Indeed, God's desire is that people of all nations should repent and be saved (2 Pet 3:9; 1 Tim 2:4).

3:7–9 Royal Decree of the King

What follows is the proclamation of a royal decree. The king of Nineveh issued an edict that concerned everyone and everything in Nineveh. The title "king of Nineveh," rather than "king of Assyria," reflects the anarchy of that period, with the powerful roles of regional governors, one of whom ruled over Nineveh.[7] The title "king of Assyria" reflects a later period when the Assyrian Empire was no longer in existence.

---

6. *HALOT* 1:64.
7. Walton, *Ancient Near Eastern Thought*, 28.

In OT narrative, ideas are emphasized either through repeated words or by elaborating on the action. The Ninevites declare a fast (3:5b); and the king and nobles emphasize the idea of fasting with their proclamation (3:7). As for the action of donning sackcloth, the outward expression of fasting, this is repeated three times:

- The Ninevites don sackcloth (3:5b);
- The king dons sackcloth (3:6); and
- A royal decree that everyone, even animals, should don sackcloth (3:8).

The royal decree has three elements: it starts with a prohibition, a negative command (3:7–8a); this is followed by a positive directive to act (3:8b); and finally, there is a wish that may function as a prayer (3:9). The decree is comprehensive, addressed to every person in the city of Nineveh, including even the animals (3:7–8). The "animals" (or "beasts") refer to wild animals; "herds or flocks" are domestic animals. All of them need to honor God as he is the dispenser of life and is able to save them (Ps 36:6).[8] In verse 7, the negative commands use specific terms related to food:[9]

- Do not let them taste;
- Do not let them eat;
- Do not let them drink.

The royal edict is marked by a beautiful parallelism, with this triplet of negatives (3:7) paralleled by the following triplet of commands to obey (3:8):

- Let people and animals be covered with sackcloth;
- Let everyone call urgently on God; and
- Let them give up their evil ways and their violence

The king's decree acknowledges that the people of Nineveh have been guilty of evil ways and acts of violence. This admission shows their humility, and their willingness to turn to God and do what is right. The decree also reveals the despair of the king and nobles, trying every possible means to cause God to hear them and be merciful to them. They urge everyone to cry out to God, and their plea for pardon is expressed both visually and audibly.

Consider the similarities between the responses and behavior of the sailors (chapter 2) and the Ninevites (chapter 4).

---

8. Tova Forti, "Of Ships and Seas, and Fish and Beasts: Viewing the Concept of Universal Providence in the Book of Jonah through the Prism of Psalms," *JSOT* 35, no. 3 (2011): 371.
9. A negative command is expressed with the negation followed by the imperfect tense of the verb. The particle "not" calls for immediate attention.

Response of the non-Israelites		
	The Sailors	**The Ninevites**
Message	The reason for the storm (1:10–12)	The destruction of Nineveh (3:4)
Action	Turning to God in prayer (1:14)	Turning to God by fasting, wearing sackcloth, royal decree, and repentance (3:5–9)
Result	The storm stops and the sailors fear the LORD (1:15–16)	No destruction (3:10)

The Ninevite king hopes that God may have compassion on them and relent (3:9). The royal decree is a wish, but it can be interpreted as a prayer as the Ninevites come before the Lord, humbly expressing their desire. People may sometimes find themselves in such a situation – seeking pardon or pleading for compassion in times of suffering but praying with a note of uncertainty. God may yet relent but no human being could ever force his hand. Nevertheless, this should not hinder any person in deep trouble from crying out to God for mercy.

3:10 RELENTING OF PUNISHMENT BY GOD

At the start of this chapter, God's merciful grace offered Jonah a second chance (3:1–2). The brief message, "Forty more days and Nineveh will be overthrown," already foretells God's mercy and compassion toward the sinful Ninevites. There is a grace period of "forty more days" for them to repent. For "Nineveh will be overthrown" is understood to be the consequential clause – warning them what would happen if they did *not* repent of their evil ways. But if they *did* repent, they would not be overthrown. Therefore, "when God saw what they did and how they turned from their evil ways, he relented and did not bring on them the destruction he had threatened" (3:10). The word "relent" appears twice in this chapter:

- The Ninevite king hopes that God may relent (3:9); and
- God relents from the destruction (3:10).

The play on words in Jonah's proclamation was already noted in the comments on 3:3–4. God's message to the Ninevites could be understand like this: the city Nineveh will be "overthrown" (destruction) if the Ninevites do not turn to God (conversion). So Jonah's proclamation announces either Nineveh's destruction – if they continue in their evil ways – or its salvation – if they demonstrate a change of heart. There is a warning of judgment, along with the promise of grace. Perhaps this contributes to the fascination of the book of Jonah, for the reader is kept in suspense at every turn of its brief chapters.

The theme of God's grace is progressively woven into each chapter. In chapter 1, from the experience of divine judgment, the sailors caught in the storm experience God's grace after they finally throw Jonah into the sea. In chapter 2, Jonah already enjoys God's saving grace while inside the belly of the fish as he repents and prays to God with petition and thanksgiving praise. Here in chapter 3, a whole nation of people and animals are saved from destruction as they all fast, pray, and cry out to God, confessing and turning away from their evil ways. Judgment is aborted and God proves himself faithful to his true nature of compassion and mercy. And chapter 4 brings us God's personal announcement of his enduring compassion and grace towards the people of Nineveh (4:11).

Jonah undoubtedly preached with great conviction about God's imminent overthrow of evil. But he probably never expected such a wicked city as Nineveh to so swiftly and sincerely repent, leading to God relenting and withholding the threatened destruction. The "success" of the prophet's preaching is tinged with irony because Jonah never sought this outcome and certainly did not welcome it! The proclamation of Jonah is like the gospel proclamation of the birth, death, and resurrection of Jesus Christ, the Son of God; and, as John reminds us, "whoever believes in him shall not perish but have eternal life" (John 3:16b).

The prophet Jonah proclaimed God's message at the right time, in the right place, and for the right people. As the Christian world celebrated 500 years of the Reformation in October 2017, some theologians reiterated how Calvin never tired of pointing out the importance of preaching the gospel to all, without prejudice or exception. In 1538, after being expelled from Geneva, Calvin felt that he was no longer fitted for pastoral ministry and planned to retire. But Martin Bucer, the great Strasbourg reformer, challenged Calvin. He pointed out that to simply hide away was to be like the runaway prophet Jonah and that Calvin, too, would end up pitiful like Jonah.[10] And so Calvin returned to ministry.

---

10. Randall C. Zachman, *John Calvin as Teacher, Pastor, and Theologian: The Shape of His Writings and Thoughts* (Grand Rapids: Baker Academic, 2006 kindle edition), 22, https://www.amazon.com/John-Calvin-Teacher-Pastor-Theologian-ebook/dp/B00D6IE0AO, accessed June 15, 2018.

Jonah

The question arises about the mass conversion of the Ninevites: Did they *all* understand the meaning and implications of the royal decree? Was everyone who complied with it really repentant and were their lives truly transformed? In other words, was their repentance both authentic and lasting?

Psychologists are interested in understanding what makes people obey or disobey orders in everyday life. In 1962, after the dreadful Holocaust under Nazi Germany – where six million Jewish people and many others in concentration camps were murdered under Adolf Hitler – Karl Adolf Eichmann, the person mainly responsible for carrying out this lethal crime, was executed. But Eichmann wrote in his jail diary, "The orders were, for me, the highest thing in my life and I had to obey them without question."[11] To find out if there was something distinctive in the German culture that caused such total and unquestioning obedience, psychologist Stanley Milgram posed this research question: "Are Germans different?"[12] His research showed that human beings were surprisingly obedient to authority. Obedience is a form of social influence, where one acts in response to a direct order from another individual, usually an authority figure. It is assumed that without such an order the person would not act in this way.[13] Conformity involves social pressure that comes from the norms imposed by the majority.

Jonah obeyed the second commission to go to Nineveh and proclaim God's message. The royal decree ordered everyone to fast and to cry out to God for mercy. All complied, but what motivated them to do so? Was it simply obedience to royal orders? Was it a desire to conform to what others in the household or community were doing? Or did the Ninevites, knowing the gravity of their plight, follow the royal decree out of repentant and submissive hearts?

A mass conversion may at times be deceptive – an individual could go along with the group without personal conviction, simply due to peer pressure, for it is not a comfortable feeling to stand out or be singled out as different. The average person tends to follow the majority so as not to be ostracized by the rest. Thus, at times of mass conversion, it is important to be aware that some may have been coerced to move with the tide of the majority. These

---

11. Allan Hall, "Eichmann Memoirs Published: Jail Diary Shows Architect of Holocaust Displayed No Remorse before 1962 Execution," https://www.theguardian.com/world/1999/aug/12/2, accessed April 18, 2019.
12. Saul McLeod, "The Milgram Shock Experience," https://www.simplypsychology.org/milgram.html, accessed April 18, 2019.
13. Saul McLeod, "Obedience to Authority," https://www.simplypsychology.org/obedience.html, accessed December 1, 2018.

people may not be genuinely repentant or sincere in their commitment, but simply be following or imitating the majority.

MODERN-DAY JONAHS AND MASS CONVERSIONS

Chapter 3 of the book of Jonah illustrates a unique revival in the city of Nineveh through Jonah's preaching. This kind of phenomenal mass conversion was replicated in the worldwide ministry of the late evangelist Billy Graham.

Billy Graham: A Man of God

On February 21, 2018, Billy Graham passed away at the age of ninety-nine. His was a matchless voice, used by God to change millions of lives, not only in America, but globally.[1] A confidant who prayed with many American presidents, from Truman to Obama, Billy was a guiding light to generations of American evangelicals. Some called him "America's pastor," while others saw him as the "Protestant pope."

Billy was a globe-trotting preacher who evangelized nearly 215 million people over six decades. He is reported to have persuaded more than 3 million people, in 185 of the world's 195 countries, to commit their lives to Christ. In 1948, when he was thirty years old, Billy and his small ministry team met for Bible study and prayer at a tiny motel in Modesto, California. He challenged the team to uphold high standards of behavior and safeguard the integrity of their ministry.

The Ministry of Billy Graham

Billy began his missionary work in 1944, speaking at rallies for the Youth for Christ Campus Life ministry. Five years later, he expanded his ministry by bringing the gospel message of tent-revival preachers into the modern media age, using any tool at his disposal – from telegrams to telephones to satellites and the Internet – to "win souls for Christ." That message, as Billy preached during thousands of altar calls, was that salvation is offered to one and all, so long as they believed in Jesus: "For God so loved the world that he gave his one and only Son, that whoever believes in him shall not perish but have eternal life" (John 3:16).

The Manila Graham Crusade: 40 Years Ago

In 1977, the Billy Graham Evangelical Association worked with the Filipino and Chinese churches at Luneta Park. I was then a first-year seminary student and felt so privileged and blessed to be able to serve at the crusade by counseling those who made the decision to accept

Jesus as their Lord and Savior. Coming from a Buddhist home, and just beginning to see how the gospel could change people's lives, I saw firsthand how people responded to the gospel, turning from hopelessness to hope in Jesus Christ. Billy's sermon would always be simple, yet complete, sincere, and solid. He would always hold a big black open Bible in one hand, lifting it up and saying, "The word of God says . . ."

The Manila Graham Crusade: After 40 years

Since 1977, the ministry of the late Billy Graham has been rooted deeply in Philippine soil for decades. In 2006, Franklin Graham, Billy's son, set foot in the Philippines and conducted evangelistic meetings outside Manila and also in the Luneta Grandstand. In February 2019, about 60,000 evangelicals and the Jesus Reigns Pentecostal churches organized a third-generation Graham Crusade conducted by Will Graham, Billy's grandson.

An Asian Gospel Crusade Evangelist

Rev. Dr. Stephen Tong, another world-renowned evangelist, is one of the few evangelists who have been as influential as Billy Graham. He is of Chinese ethnicity and resides in Jakarta, Indonesia. Through his ministry, Rev. Tong, who is rooted in Reformed theology, has reached out to an estimated 29 million people.[2] Called to bring the gospel of Christ at the age of 17, he travels to many countries around the world, with the objectives of removing barriers to Christian faith and leading people to Christ. Today, even in his advanced years, he continues traveling to four different countries in Asia almost every week for theological symposiums and speaking engagements. This is in addition to his other trips around the globe all year long.

There are countless new believers who are the fruits of these international gospel crusades. Many faithful pastors serving our Lord today are also the products of the revival messages given at these evangelistic nights.

Chapter 3 of the book of Jonah reminds us that our Lord's Great Commission is calling followers not only to go and persuade unbelievers, but also for Jesus's followers to go and "make disciples" of all nations. These disciples are to become disciple-makers for the expansion of God's kingdom. The delivery of God's powerful word by his faithful messengers will go forth and bear fruit, resulting in transformed lives. The book of Isaiah affirms this: "As the rain and the snow come down from heaven, and do not return to it without watering the earth and making it bud and flourish, so that it yields seed for the sower and bread for the eater, so is my word that goes out from my mouth: It will not return to

Jonah 3:1 – 4:11

me empty, but will accomplish what I desire and achieve the purpose for which I sent it" (Isa 55:10–11).

---

1. Daniel Burke, "Billy Graham, Whose 'Matchless Voice Changed the Lives of Millions,' Dies at 99," https://edition.cnn.com/2018/02/21/us/billy-graham-obit/index.html, accessed February 21, 2018.
2. "Critical Stephen Tong: Reckoning Rev. Dr. Stephen Tong's Message and His Version of Reformed Theology in a Wider Theological Context," https://students.wts.edu/stayinformed/view.html?id=161, accessed May 6, 2018.

4:1–11 RAGING AGAINST GOD'S COMPASSION

Growing up in a big family in metropolitan Manila was never easy for Bong. His parents belonged to the first wave of Chinese immigrants who came to the Philippines around the early 1960s. After years of toil, and many trials, Bong's hardworking father finally became the owner of a medium-sized supermarket. Still, life was not easy, especially at the start. But Bong's father lived and worked with integrity and industry. His good reputation enabled him to borrow enough money for Bong and all his siblings to finish college. Before the start of each school year, Bong's father would go to a well-to-do relative and trade post-dated checks for cash so that he could pay his children's tuition. Bong's father would see to it that all his debts were paid before the due date. Thus he earned the reputation of being a man of his word. He was also known to be kind and generous to anyone in need.

Bong, now an adult, helps out in his father's supermarket business. But he gets into frequent arguments over his father's seemingly limitless patience with their customers. Some customers have IOUs that are overdue by two months, yet Bong's father continues to be merciful when they beg for a few more weeks to settle up. When Bong protests, his father reminds him that just as kindness has been dispensed to their family, they too must show kindness to others. Bong reacts with impatience, and even anger: "Nonsense! Might as well give them all our wares as gifts!" Bong often criticizes his father: "Dad, you are allowing these lazy customers to take advantage of your kindness!" Bong's kind-hearted, tender-spirited father tries to calm him down; he says gently, "It is better to be taken advantage of than to take advantage of others." Bong's father is a great example of a man with a generous heart.

In the NIV, this final chapter of Jonah's narrative is entitled, "Jonah's anger at the LORD's compassion." Jonah's anger comes on the heels of the amazing success of his mission in Nineveh. The whole city of Nineveh had repented and turned to God. Jonah's anger is unbecoming, even unbelievable. In the first place, it is unfitting that a prophet of God should rage against the Lord in this manner. Second, how could Jonah rant and rave after he himself had been given a second chance by God? Jonah's story does not end with chapter 3 as the grand finale, with a triumphant shout of "mission accomplished!" In this last chapter lies the key to why Jonah began by fleeing from God's call in chapter 1. It also teaches an important truth – that God's compassion embraces *all* humankind, not just his prophet Jonah and not just the Jewish people.

The conversation between Jonah and his God is an I-Thou communication. God's disobedient prophet (1:1–16) – saved by God (1:17 – 2:10) and given a second chance by God (3:1–10) – now responds by showing his dissatisfaction and displeasure towards God (4:1–11). The chapter has three sections: Jonah's reproach against God's compassion (4:1–2); Jonah's request to die (4:3–9); and God's reproof of Jonah (4:10–11).

Here are some points to ponder in relation to the wrestling match between Jonah and the Lord God in chapter 4.

Person in Focus	Jonah	The Lord God
Speech	Argument (4:2–3)	Explanation (4:10–11)
Action	Anger (4:5)	Compassion (4:6a)
Response	Happiness (4:6b)	Provision (4:7–8)
Speech	Death wish (4:9b)	Questioning (4:9a)

4:1–2 Reproaching God

The true state of Jonah's heart, revealed in the final chapter of the narrative, surprises the reader with yet another twist in the tale. Jonah, who seemed dutifully obedient in chapter 3, now responds to the success of his mission with unexpected bitterness and anger towards God.

Chapter 4 begins, "But to Jonah this seemed very wrong, and he became angry" (4:1), literally, "the great wickedness was evil to Jonah." In other words, the events of chapter 3, specifically the fact that God had relented, irritates and exasperates Jonah. He considers this a great injustice – "this seemed very wrong" (1:1a) – and so "he became angry" (1:1b). The verb used here is "anger was kindled to him," which means that he was angry and that this anger was expressed in feelings of grief and sadness. The verb "*harah*" ("irritate") is related both to an Aramaic root meaning "quarrel" and to an Arabic root meaning "burning."[14] The action verb depicts his angry emotions. Jonah has worked himself up into a fury because Nineveh was spared God's punishment.

To further describe his rage, the narrative uses the adjective "great" (*gadol*) to convey Jonah's displeasure. The book of Jonah uses this root word fifteen times as either a noun, an adjective, or a verb. Except for two instances where the noun represents the people (3:5, 7) and one occasion where the verb states an action (4:10), the remaining twelve appearances emphasize the extent to which the matter affects Jonah:

- Nineveh, the "great" (*gadol*) city (1:2; 3:1; 4:11)
- "Great" (*gadol*) wind (1:4)
- "Violent" or "great" (*gadol*) storm (1:4, 12)
- "Greatly" (*gadol*) feared (1:10, 16)
- "Huge" (*gadol*) fish (1:17; MT 2:1)
- "Great" (*gadol*) city (3:3)
- From the "greatest" (*gadol*) to the least (3:5)
- The king and his "nobles" (*gadol*) (3:7)
- Great (*gadol*) anger (4:1)
- Great (*gadol*) pleasure (4:6)[15]
- Make it "grow" (*gadol*) (4:10)

Why does the repentance of the Ninevites kindle such fierce anger in Jonah? When God responds without wrath against the Ninevites, Jonah interprets this as "wrong" or "evil" (*ra'ah*). The Ninevites repented of their evil ways, but now Jonah's response is evil.

It is interesting to see how the word "evil" (*ra'ah*) is used in the book of Jonah:

- the "wickedness" (*ra'ah*) of the Ninevites (1:2)
- the "calamity" (*ra'ah*) at sea (1:7)
- the "trouble" (*ra'ah*) that Jonah may be responsible for (1:8)
- the "evil" (*ra'ah*) ways the Ninevites are to give up (3:8)
- God sees their repentance from their "evil" (*ra'ah*) ways (3:10a)

---

14. BDB 354a; *HALOT* 1:351a.
15. Although NIV translates this "very happy," the Hebrew text uses *gadol* ("great").

- God relents from the "destruction" (*ra'ah*) he had threatened (3:10b)
- Very wrong (*ra'ah*) (4:1)
- God relents from sending "calamity" (*ra'ah*) (4:2)
- Jonah's discomfort (*ra'ah*) (4:6)

In his anger, Jonah's prayer turns into an argument with God: "Isn't this what I said, LORD, when I was still at home? That is what I tried to forestall by fleeing to Tarshish. I knew that you are a gracious and compassionate God, slow to anger and abounding in love, a God who relents from sending calamity" (4:2). Jonah's own words reveal the reason for his disobedience in rejecting God's commission by fleeing to Tarshish (1:3). He fears the repentance of Nineveh and God's deliverance of Israel's enemy more than he fears for his own life.[16] Like an unruly, insubordinate teenager, unable to keep up his pretensions any longer, Jonah bursts out with his real feelings. He argues like an unmanageable adolescent, adamant and defiant in presenting and defending his own views.

Previously, readers were kept in the dark as to why Jonah fled from God, for chapter 1 did not recount any conversation with God. But now we read, "Is this not what I said, LORD, when I was still at home?" (4:2a). Jonah rationalizes that he tried to flee to Tarshish because he knew that God's nature – "gracious and compassionate . . . slow to anger and abounding in love" – would cause him to relent from bringing calamity (4:2b); he even admits that he wanted to "forestall" what God was trying to accomplish. Jonah uses two verbs to describe his flight to Tarshish: "I was so *quick* to *flee* to Tarshish." The second word *barah* ("fleeing") is always translated "to flee." The first word *qadam* ("quick" or "anticipates") has a different interpretation as it could also mean, "to be in front," "to confront," or "to anticipate."[17] Thus, the phrase can be translated, "I ran so fast as to flee." The simple meaning is that he was quick to act. Another possibility is, "That is why I wanted to *contest* you by fleeing to Tarshish." Jonah wanted to prevent the outcome of God's mercy by challenging God. The last possible translation is, "That is what I anticipated by fleeing to Tarshish." This would mean that he foresaw God's action and is trying to justify his own response.

---

16. Ma Man Iong, "Shall God Not Also Pity . . .? Relational Divine Mission on the Book of Jonah from the Perspective of Genesis 1–3" (MA Thesis, Luther Seminary, 2013), 46.
17. BDB 869b–870a; *HALOT* 3:1068b–1069a.

In both his attitudes and his actions, Jonah is engaged in a wrestling match with God. In effect, Jonah is asserting, "See, I told you so when I was still at home," adding, rather presumptuously, "I have tried to *prevent* you, God, from relenting in your judgment upon the Ninevites, so I fled to Tarshish; but I failed, and now it is happening! I know it is your nature to be loving and forgiving, so I do not want to be a part of your mercy kindness to Nineveh."

Verse 2, which explains why Jonah is so angry about the outcome of his mission, forms the backbone of Jonah's story. Embodied in this one verse is also a key theological doctrine of who God is and how and why he does what he sovereignly does. It is ironic that the messenger of God is able to anticipate God's being and doing so accurately yet would rather not be part of the success of the mission.

These attributes of God which Jonah affirms (4:2) are drawn from God's self-revelation in Exodus 34:6–7. Moses also refers to these qualities in his prayer on behalf of the people (Num 14:18). In some contexts, God's compassion or being "slow to anger" affirms his patience (Pss 85:5; 103:8; Joel 2:13). Joel's words are similar to Jonah 4:2, but their purpose is very different. In the book of Joel, the Lord appeals to the people, through the prophet, to repent because of these attributes; in the book of Jonah, however, the prophet is complaining against these attributes.[18] Joel appeals to the people to return to a God who "relents from sending calamity"; Jonah, however, grumbles against a God who "relents from sending calamity."

The following comparison shows that the passage may be applied beyond Jonah's selfish restriction of the text to Israel:

Exodus 34:6	Jonah 4:2
And he passed in front of Moses, proclaiming,	I knew that you are
"The Lord, the Lord, the compassionate and gracious God, slow to anger, abounding in love and faithfulness"	a gracious and compassionate God, slow to anger, and abounding in love, a God who relents from sending calamity

---

18. For the positive and negative aspects of God's action in forgiving and punishing, see Joseph Too Shao, and Rosa Ching Shao, *Joel, Nahum & Malachi*, ABC (Manila: Asia Theological Association, 2013), 53. In intertextual studies, some scholars interpret Jonah's quotation of God's attributes as reacting to Joel's preaching; see Annette Schellenberg, "An Anti-Prophet among the Prophets? On the Relationship of Jonah to Prophecy," *JSOT* 39 (2015): 358.

It seems that Jonah had a problem with the recipients of God's divine mercy. Thus, many tend to view Jonah as outright selfish and even narcissistic.[19] Jonah's creedal formula of God's compassion as abounding is one thing; his personal understanding and practice of God's compassion, however, prove to be limited, narrowly focused on his own country and his own people. Jonah was expecting, even anticipating, Nineveh's destruction, and thus opposed divine forgiveness for these enemies of his native land.

We see four kinds of prayer in the book of Jonah. In chapter 1, the pagan sailors cry out to their own gods, and later to the Lord God, for help. This is a prayer of supplication; and similar supplications are found in the book of Psalms. In chapter 2, Jonah utters thanksgiving praise while inside the belly of the fish, affirming his trust in God's salvation; we find many prayers of thanksgiving in the Psalms, too. In chapter 3, the Ninevites, from royalty to the lowest ranks, fast and pray, vowing to turn away from their evil ways; such prayers of confession are common in the Psalms. Finally, in chapter 4, the prophet laments that he would rather die than live. This resembles the songs of lament found in the book of Psalms.[20]

Before getting further into Jonah's argument with God, it is worth exploring why Jonah was reluctant to see his mission accomplished and why he was so violently opposed to the Ninevites being spared God's judgment. Consider these possibilities:

- Perhaps, in Jonah's eyes, the Ninevites deserved to be condemned for their evil and violence against his own people, the Israelites. *Nationalism* may have called Jonah to be loyal to his own country.
- A strong sense of justice may have caused Jonah's misgivings about seeing such evil go unpunished and blinded him to God's mercy and loving kindness.
- Perhaps Jonah just could not accept the truth that God loves people of other tribes and races, not just his own. Reluctance to share God's compassion with others reflects his egoism, the self-interest that characterized his ministry. Racial *ethnocentricism,* the belief that one's ethnic group is superior to another, would have

---

19. Moberly, "Educating Jonah," 199, 205.
20. For a discussion on the genre of lament, see Federico G. Villanueva, "Preaching Lament," in *Reclaiming the Old Testament for Christian Preaching*, eds. Grenville J. R. Kent, Paul J. Kissling and Laurence A. Turner (Downers Grove: IVP Academic, 2010), 64–84.

prevented him from viewing other nations positively, as recipients of God's gracious love.

- Jonah may have feared the shame that would follow if his preaching did not accomplish its purpose. Here, the five-word proclamation of Jonah, "Forty more days and Nineveh will be overthrown," is taken as announcing that the great city of Nineveh will be destroyed within forty days. So if God did *not* destroy Nineveh, then Jonah's prophecy would fail and be void. In Mosaic law, the fulfillment of a prophetic message is a test of the credibility of a prophet and Jonah may have feared the shame of being labeled a false prophet by his own people or even killed as a result of unfulfilled prophecy (Deut 18:20–22). Jonah may have wondered what fate awaited him once he returned home to his people. No wonder he is not keen to go home. Instead, he intends to sit at the eastern city gate to see what would happen next, once the forty days had passed. *Self-centeredness* and *egocentrism* may have prevented Jonah from appreciating the greater picture of God's graciousness.

Honor-shame themes are inherent in many biblical stories, in both the OT (Gen 2:2–3; 38:26; Deut 5:16; Esth 1:15–20; Ezra 9:6–15; Pss 4:2–3; 25:13; 74:1–4; Prov 13:18; Zeph 3:19) and NT (Luke 9:2–27; Rom 6:1–7; 8:1–18; 2 Cor 4:7–12; 2 Peter 2). The term "shame" and its derivatives occur nearly three hundred times in the OT and forty-five times in the NT.[21] The biblical teaching about honor and shame reminds us that the very heartbeat of God is about saving humanity from shame and restoring honor. God's will is carried out and God's glory is revealed in the ministry of Jonah, despite the self-centeredness of God's messenger.

In recent decades, shame as a complex emotional construct has generated significant interest in the fields of psychology, sociology, anthropology, and even neurobiology. Some researchers make distinctions between different types of shame, such as traditional shame, Western versus Eastern shame, individualistic shame, sex and shame, and shame-filled opportunity.[22] In one study focusing on shame in relation to false self and narcissism, shame is linked to

---

21. Jayson Georges, "Why Has Nobody Told Me This Before? The Gospel the World Is Waiting For," *Mission Frontiers* (Jan-Feb 2015): 7–10.
22. Andy Crouch, "The Return of Shame," 33–41.

the experience of the self – a failure of the whole or global self, that is, the self of the person is the focus of evaluation as evidence of shame.[23] It is said that shame is regarded as the most self-reflecting of emotions. Subsequent self-evaluation in terms of being useless, defective, powerless, or a misfit could place the person in a state of isolation. This raging shame – fury, coupled with a deep sense of shame – could have been what Jonah was experiencing. He does not return home but waits in seclusion.

Is There a Jonah Inside Us?

As we ponder Jonah's failure to appreciate God's heart of compassion and grace, we may either sympathize with Jonah's pain and hurt or criticize his unbecoming behavior as God's messenger. But it is important to shift the focus of Jonah and zoom in on ourselves, asking: Is there a Jonah inside us? The Sunday School song, *I Don't Want to Be a Jonah,* rings in my heart every time I think about Jonah. No mature Christian *wants* to be a Jonah, but is there an unwitting Jonah lurking inside us? As we reflect again on Jonah's story, this time, let's also search our own hearts.

Looking back at chapter 1, we can agree with Jonah in his perfect proclamation of his creed of allegiance to God: "I am a Hebrew and I worship the Lord, the God of heaven, who made the sea and the dry land" (1:9). What a wonderful and powerful belief, yet Jonah had fled from this God and the mission assigned to him. Have we, like Jonah, proudly professed our faith, only to live lives that are weak in faith?

Tracing Jonah's journey in chapter 2, we hear him loud and clear inside the belly of the fish, praying to God, petitioning for divine help in a distressful situation, and making promises to "sacrifice" with "grateful praise." Do we tend to call upon the Lord God only, or primarily, in times of crisis? Have we made personal vows, only to forget our promises once the crisis was past?

In chapter 3, we see Jonah doing exactly as he was told, going to the Ninevites and preaching God's message just as God had commanded. While we may speak and preach God's word, with what motives do we do so? Our mouths may agree with the Scriptures, but only God sees our heart. Do we sometimes preach to put on a show, rather than with integrity before our audience of one?

---

23. Akumsungla Aier, "Relationship of Object Relations: Shame and Narcissism to Adolescents' False Self Behavior on Social Network Sites," Doctoral diss. (Asia Graduate School of Theology, Philippines, 2018), 49, 53.

Continuing to scrutinize and search our inner heart, soul, and mind, we come to the last chapter. The prophet cannot wait any longer to express his anger before God. Once again, Jonah gets his doctrine right as he recites a credo about God's goodness: "You are a gracious and compassionate God, slow to anger and abounding in love, a God who relents from sending calamity" (4:2).[24] He knows his theology so well! He has perfect head knowledge of God, yet his heart is not receptive to transformation by God. Today, many preachers and pastors have attained theological degrees but are they helping to deliver God's word from the listeners' heads to their hearts? As followers of our Lord God, are we constantly asking ourselves this soul-searching question: How do I get my faith from my head to my heart?

Most of us probably do harbor something of a Jonah inside us. Jeremiah warns of the deceitfulness of our own hearts (Jer 17:9), and "Knowledge puffs up while love builds up" (1 Cor 8:1b) is a timely reminder for all preachers. The need to synchronize our *talk* (faith) with our *walk* (deeds) is a teaching found throughout the Scriptures (2 Tim 2:15, 24; Titus 2:7–8; Jas 2:20–24; 1 John 2:6).

4:3–9 Requesting Death

Stubbornly refusing to leave the city, Jonah remains on its outskirts near the countryside. As he waits to see what will happen next, he wrestles with God. Three times he asks God to just let him die (4:3, 8, 9). Jonah's silent "no" of chapter 1 now becomes a suicidal "no."

In verse 3, Jonah continues his heated prayer. Having spewed out the reason he is angry about God's grace towards Nineveh, he now demands that God just let him die. Jonah prays for a quick and drastic solution to appease his growing displeasure with the outcome of his mission: "Now, LORD, take away my life, for it is better for me to die than to live" (4:3). In other words, "Take my life from me, LORD, for death is better to me than life." Jonah is brusque, revealing a heart that is turning away or distancing itself from God. Anger in itself is not a sin. The feeling of anger is actually a God-given emotion; it is the way we act on such feelings that determines whether our anger will become sinful or helpful.[25] Nevertheless, anger is just one letter short of

---

24. This credo on God's goodness is mentioned seven times in Scripture: Exod 34:6–7; Neh 9:17; Pss 86:15; 103:8; 145:8; Joel 2:13; Jonah 4:2.
25. Rosa C. Shao, "Anger Management or Mismanagement: When It Thunders, It Roars or Rolls," in *Expanding Horizons: Theological Reflections*, eds. Joseph T. Shao, Rosa C. Shao and Jean Uayan (Valenzuela: Biblical Seminary of the Philippines, 2010), 120.

danger! The biblical sage counsels, "Fools give full vent to their rage, but the wise bring calm in the end" (Prov 29:11). The underlying intent behind the expression or explosion of anger is usually one of the following: (a) a real or perceived attack on one's self-worth; (b) a threat to one's basic needs; or (c) the need to defend one's basic convictions.

God responds to Jonah's pouting request with a question: "Is it right for you to be angry?" (4:4). Jonah is upset, and not yet ready to answer the Lord, so he does not respond until the question is asked again in verse 9. With his probing question, the Lord God is inviting Jonah to dialogue. The Lord God is compassionate towards the Ninevites because he desires to save them, but he is equally concerned with correcting Jonah's perspective. Is it appropriate for Jonah to be infuriated with God's merciful actions? Evidently, the correct answer should be "no." God's question demonstrates his patience with Jonah, or anyone else, who dares challenge him with foolish and short-sighted arguments. The Lord God is truly "a gracious and compassionate God, slow to anger and abounding in love" (4:2).

Jonah is back in wrestling mode. Like an argumentative adolescent – who considers that his rights have been violated and that his view is the only right one – Jonah simply turns a deaf ear and walks away from the conversation. Fleeing the city, he holes up in a self-made shelter, and waits to see what will happen next.

Does Jonah really mean it when he asks God to let him die? What kind of challenge is Jonah throwing at a loving God? Is this some kind of emotional blackmail? Jonah is once again behaving like a spoilt teenager, testing the limits of his parents' love, sulkily insisting that they do not love him unless they give in to his request.

But deep within Jonah's heart, he apparently senses God's gracious and compassionate love, from the moment of his rebellious runaway voyage right up to the present moment. He knew it was God's hand that caused the storm at sea (1:12). When thrown overboard, he experienced the saving hand of God placing him inside the belly of the fish (2:1) and later, bringing him safely to dry land (2:10). When he accepts the assignment to preach to Nineveh, a city full of evil and violence, he is kept safe in God's care (3:3–4). Yet now he claims that he would rather be dead than watch the Ninevites rejoicing in their freedom from God's condemnation. Nevertheless, Jonah's decision to tarry at the city border may point to an ambivalent attitude towards his own death. He plans to wait out the forty days, perhaps to see if the Ninevites would return to their evil ways. In short, Jonah may not really want to die, at least not just yet. Persistent and headstrong, he continues his wrestling match with God.

Jonah chose to run away from the great revival going on in Nineveh. He probably regrets returning to proclaim God's message there and wishes he had just kept running! But as much as the Lord God would not allow Jonah to run away to Tarshish, neither will leave him to hide away and sulk in his make-shift shelter outside the city. In spite of Jonah's ranting, and despite his sulky refusal to engage in conversation, God loves the unrepentant Jonah as much as he loves the repentant Ninevites. Having already given Jonah a second chance, when he could easily have sent another willing messenger, God will not allow Jonah's silence or distance to stand in the way now. The Lord God is more interested in building up the man Jonah than in the success of Jonah's ministry. God's objective is to help Jonah understand the gracious and compassionate nature of God. Initially, God's intervention is non-verbal – verses 6, 7, and 8 use the silent action word "provided." Just as God "provided" the big fish to swallow Jonah (1:17), he will now teach his prophet by means of object lessons involving a plant, a worm, and a scorching wind.

Miraculously, a leafy plant sprouts over Jonah, giving him shade for his head and easing his discomfort. This vine could have been a local climbing plant or a plant with large leaves. What is miraculous is not the plant itself but the amazing speed at which it grows. This plant (*qiqayon*) is identified as a "gourd," "castor-oil plant," or "ivy."[26] For the first time in the narrative, Jonah is "very happy." The descriptive word *gadol* (great) is used fifteen times in these four short chapters, in the form of a superlative. Perhaps Jonah may have felt that this suddenly-growing shrub, soothing and calming him, was a sign of God's pleasure with him. This delights him, but not for long.

At dawn the next day, God provides a worm, which chews the plant so that it withers away. And then, as the sun rises, God appoints a scorching east wind which brings the blazing sun over Jonah's head. The heat is so searing that Jonah almost faints. Unable to bear the sudden sweltering atmosphere, Jonah again expresses his desire to die, in almost the same words as before: "It would be better for me to die than to live" (3:8).

The purpose of God's object lessons is to show Jonah that the shielding vine tree, the hungry worm, the blistering wind, and the scorching heat – just like the lots and the big fish in chapter 1 – all respond promptly to God's command. Jonah, however, remains conflicted with the Lord and refuses to respond to his love.

---

26. H. W. Wolff, *Obadiah and Jonah: A Commentary* (Minneapolis: Augsburg, 1986), 169–170.

IS GOD PLAYING GAMES WITH HIS PEOPLE?

Is God Playing Games with Jonah?
Does God delight in giving Jonah a few brief moments of bliss, only to replace these with misery? Is God playing a trick on Jonah, blessing him with the vine plant one moment and then taking it away so soon? Is God truly good and kind to humankind?

Sometimes, it is very hard to understand God's ways. Amid natural calamities and disasters of great magnitude, we may harbor doubts about God's goodness. At such times it is difficult to confidently declare, "Naked I came from my mother's womb, and naked I will depart. The LORD gave and the LORD has taken away; may the name of the LORD be praised" (Job 1:21). When bad things happen to us, the devil would like us to become resentful toward the Lord God.

Is God Fooling Abraham with His Promise?
One morning, during my devotions, I read Genesis 21–24. In Abraham's and Sarah's old age, when all hopes of having a child had grown dim, the Lord was gracious to them. At the promised time Isaac, the son of the promise, was born (Gen 21:1–3). Isaac's name means "he laughs," and this child brought laughter to everyone who heard this great news.

Then came the time when Abraham's faith in God was sorely tested: "Take your son, your only son, whom you love – Isaac – and go to the region of Moriah. Sacrifice him there as a burnt offering on a mountain I will show you" (Gen 22:2). What is God trying to do? Why would God fulfill a promise and then take away the son of this promise? Is God fooling Abraham with his promise?

God wanted to see whether Abraham truly trusted in God's faithfulness to his promise. And Abraham passed the divine test with flying colors. The incident with Isaac reveals the genuineness and depth of Abraham's faith in God, and it is this faith that God "credited to him as righteousness" (Gen 15:6). The apostle Paul strongly argues for righteousness by faith – and not by circumcision or any human deed or work – so that "those who rely on faith are blessed along with Abraham, the man of faith" (Gal 3:9).

God is not in the business of playing games or fooling his followers. As with Abraham and Jonah, God may sometimes test our faith. When he does, how will we fare: Will our faith stand the challenge of total obedience? Or will it fall apart because we give in to fear or doubt God's faithfulness?

4:10–11 Reproved by God

God asked Jonah, "Is it right for you to be angry about the plant?" (4:9a). The brief dialogue that follows highlights the contrast between God and Jonah. In verse 4, God questions the justice of Jonah's anger over the salvation of the Ninevites. Here in verse 9, God questions the justice of Jonah's anger over the destruction of the plant. It is a direct confrontation between God and Jonah, a tug-of-war of words.

The conflict between Jonah and the Lord is based around the prophet's request to die. It is a twisted explanation of reality.[27] God has saved Jonah with the fish and brought him out alive; for Jonah to vehemently ask God to let him die is like Jonah twisting the reality of his existence. This also implies more underlying issues to unearth between God's loving kindness and Jonah's displeasure of God's saving action. God could have let Jonah stay in the sea, face distress, and ultimately drown. God could have let Jonah die at his first utterance of a death wish. Instead, God has graciously given Jonah the space and time to think through the events that have taken place; and Jonah must surely have seen how God's hand has been patiently and lovingly drawing him back to God since the day he took off to Tarshish. Now the Lord God will explain the meaning behind his object lesson: the plant. God makes it clear that Jonah has no rights and no say in respect of this plant that had brought him such joy. Jonah argues for his right to be angry, but God asserts that he has no such right since he has done nothing to care for it or make it grow.

The vine plant that God prepares for Jonah brings him such joy that when God takes it away, Jonah no longer finds a reason to live, but just wants to run away from the presence of God and from all that is happening around him. Jonah had seemed quite prepared to stay put and enjoy the plant from God since it provided consoling shade. Now that this relief has been removed, Jonah is angry enough to die. How easy, too, for many of us to enjoy God's gifts, yet neglect to enjoy our Lord God, the giver of all things good and beautiful and, at times, even seemingly bad and ugly. Like ignorant, short-sighted children, we may live simply for the gifts and overlook the giver of these gifts.

---

27. Rob Barrett, "Meaning More than They Say," 239.

WHEN SUICIDAL THOUGHTS LOOM[1]

It is generally accepted that life is hard; and for many, life just keeps getting harder, regardless of age, gender, race, economic status, or even religion and faith. Recently, two prominent American celebrities took their own lives within a week. Kate Spade, whose uniquely designed bags sold well because they make people happy, and Anthony Bourdain, whose travels and encounters with exotic cuisine brought delight to food connoisseurs and his audience, were both found dead in apparent suicides. So we ask ourselves, "Why do people who have it all, end it all?" Kate's husband, Andy, admitted that his wife had been suffering from severe depression, and that they had been living separately although with no plans of divorce. He added: "There was no indication and no warning."[2] Anthony Bourdain's case shocked his worldwide viewers who felt they had lost a friend.[3] Barely a month before these two incidents, thirty-year-old megachurch pastor Andrew Stoecklein took his own life after an open battle with depression and anxiety, leaving behind his wife Kayla and their three sons.

Suicide is a raging epidemic, not only in America but globally. It is the tragic and lethal culmination of a psychological process resulting from unresolved events that create depression and hopelessness.[4] It is reportedly the second leading cause of death among fifteen-to-nineteen-year-olds. However, many suicides are not officially recorded due to the stigma of dishonor; many of these are disguised as accidents instead. The suicide rate in the Philippines is lower than that of many other countries – for instance, China, Japan, Republic of Korea, and Sri Lanka.[5] Nevertheless, it is alarming that figures have risen steadily in the Philippines over the twenty-year-period from 1992 to 2012. Research states that in 2012 alone as many as seven Filipinos took their own lives every day, a troubling rate of one suicide every three-and-a-half hours.[6]

Why Do Such Things Happen?
The Bible contains accounts of some great spiritual servants who were used mightily by God. Ironically, even some of them cried out to God praying to die. We have Moses, overcome by the burden of a disgruntled people (Num 11:11–15) and Elijah, discouraged and downcast, seeing himself as the only one standing for God (1 Kgs 19:4–5). We also have Jonah, with his self-centered indignation, dismayed over God's mercy for his nation's enemies (Jonah 4:3, 8–9); the disobedient King Saul, whose distorted outlook changed him from a national hero to a national disgrace (1 Sam 10:22–27; 31:4); and of course there is Judas

Iscariot, the disciple who betrayed Jesus, whose sense of hopelessness may have driven him to take his own life (Matt 27:5; Acts 1:18–19).

Every suicide is actually a cry for help. As we see from biblical examples as well as contemporary cases, a combination of faulty reasoning and a deep sense of hopelessness lies at the core of the struggle with suicide. An overwhelming sense of sadness is almost always a key warning sign.[7] Suicide is often related to serious depression. Disappointment with others, with ourselves, and even with God may create depressive moods of varying degrees of seriousness. At the core of depression is not just a feeling of helplessness and hopelessness but also the experience of loss. There are three kinds of loss: (a) actual loss, as in the death of a loved one; (b) abstract loss, as in not receiving an expected and deserved promotion; and (c) threatened loss, as in probable physical illness or the likelihood of failing in one's studies. Usually, several factors combine to cause people to contemplate suicide. When God's children experience feelings of desperation, desolation, self-doubt, self-hate, or self-pity, the devil may use these to provoke suicidal and morbid thoughts.

One reason for choosing to kill oneself is in an attempt to escape a life of deep loneliness, of feeling overwhelmed by human frailty. Another reason might be to ease one's emotional pain. Teenagers may attempt suicide because they have failed exams or feel heartbroken over broken relationships. Others may resort to such drastic action in an attempt to escape intolerable conflicts in personal relationships or deeply painful inner wounds. One such unseen, even unconscious, wound within could be caused by layers upon layers of shame, which find their roots in early relationships and experiences. At the heart of such a wound is the sense of shame which says, "*I am* no good," as opposed to guilt which acknowledges, "What I *did* was not good."[8] In other words, shame says, "I am bad," whereas guilt says, "I did that bad thing."

Shame is typically characterized by feelings of inferiority and worthlessness, leading to a desire to escape or disappear. One's entire self is suddenly devalued by shame.[9] The Chinese idiom 老羞成怒 (*lao xiu cheng nu*) points to shame as a stimulus for rage, especially among men. This idiomatic expression connotes a level of shame so deep that it turns to anger as a coping mechanism for survival. This raging shame may initially be directed outward against others. But it could also turn inward, against oneself, leading to depression and suicidal thoughts – like dark, dreary, and deadly clouds hovering over a person.

What to Do When Facing Suicidal Thoughts?

Anyone could be troubled by suicidal thoughts. This is most likely to happen when one's defense mechanisms and means of support are weakened under pressure during stressful times. Due to the limitations of space in this article, the following are just a few simple suggestions for dealing with such thoughts and feelings. Note that it is important to seek medical professional help if needed.

Tell someone you trust about your feelings. It is a great relief to talk things through with a safe person. Consider how God talked with Moses, Elijah, and Jonah in their moments of distress and depression. Talk to a friend, or go to your pastor or teacher, and of course, talk to God himself for he is always waiting to hear you.

Take action. Use some of these personal self-help strategies: (a) catch those gloomy thoughts and feelings, and rebuke them with facts and truths from reality and God's word; (b) keep a journal and write out your thoughts, replacing the negative ones with more positive perspectives; (c) listen to uplifting Christian music; and (d) cultivate healthy and helpful habits such as going for a walk, exercising in a gym, or enjoying a cup of tea with a friend.

Thank God for everything that comes your way, be it good or bad. The apostle Paul instructs and invites us to "Rejoice always, pray continually, give thanks in all circumstances; for this is God's will for you in Christ Jesus" (1 Thess 5:16–18). The book of Psalms is rich in examples of God's people choosing to trust the Lord God in their weakness and woes. David, for example, affirmed, "No one who hopes in you will ever be put to shame" (Ps 25:3); he chose to "wait for the Lord" (Ps 27:14a) and the Lord turned his "wailing into dancing" so that his heart might sing God's praises (Ps 30:11–12). The psalms speak frequently of thank offerings (Pss 50:14; 56:12). Give thanks no matter what, for "Gratitude makes sense of our past, brings peace for today, and creates a vision for tomorrow."[10]

Ways of Helping Others in This Deadly Troubled State

So often, when a friend is under overwhelming stress, significant people close to him may say, "He is strong enough to handle it." Beware! He may well handle it by killing himself. Suicide is, without doubt, a counselor's greatest fear. Parents, teachers, and particularly counselors working in schools, churches, community mental health, and private practice should take steps to assess the likelihood of clients – whether teens or adults – acting on their suicidal thoughts.

The assessment begins with a straightforward question: "Have you had any thoughts of harming yourself?" The belief that this is planting the idea of suicide in a client's head is a myth.[11] The underlying message of any effective suicide intervention must be, "I care about you and I take you seriously." Explore the person's personal history, discover the plan for self-harm, and clear the home of easily available lethal materials. It is helpful to make a written contract – to have your friend or client formally sign an agreement to contact you if he or she has suicidal feelings. You must be available at all times and provide a suicide hotline or counselor as a backup when you cannot be available. This conveys to them that their lives are important to you. Refer suicidal clients or teens to more competent counselors if the person becomes more out of control or increasingly suicidal.

Concluding Thoughts

Suicide is generally the result of some form of depression, stemming from loss of some kind – loss of a loved one, a position, finances, status, self-worth, and so on. It is important to meditate on the circumstances of the loss and to recognize that if God has allowed this loss, then he can use it to bring growth and to deepen our relationship with him.

Whenever we experience shame as a disturbing feeling in our lives, we can look to God's saving grace in Christ Jesus for encouragement. Our Lord Jesus bore and took upon himself all of our shame and guilt. In Christ, there is no more condemnation, no more shame. In suicide intervention, hear and share our Lord's powerful words: "I have told you these things, so that in me you may have peace. In this world you will have trouble. But take heart! I have overcome the world" (John 16:33).

---

1. Expanded from Rosa C. Shao, "When Suicidal Thoughts Loom," *BSOP in Focus* 103 (October-December 2018): 1–3.
2. Vanessa Friedman, "Andy Spade on Kate's Death: 'There Was No Indication and No Warning,'" https://www.nytimes.com/2018/06/06/style/kate-spade-husband-andy-spade.html, accessed June 29, 2018.
3. Brian Stelter, "CNN's Anthony Bourdain Dead at 61," https://edition.cnn.com/2018/06/08/us/anthony-bourdain-obit/index.html, accessed June 29, 2018.
4. Tim Clinton and Ron Hawkins, *The Quick-Reference Guide to Biblical Counseling* (Grand Rapids: Baker Books, 2009), 254.
5. Herbert Hendin, Lakshmi Vijayuakumar, José M. Bertolote, Hong Wang, Michael R. Phillips, Jane Pirkis, "Epidemiology of Suicide in Asia," https://www.who.int/mental_health/resources/suicide_prevention_asia_chapter1.pdf?ua=1, accessed May 11, 2019.
6. Joel Ruiz Butuyan, "Seven Filipinos Commit Suicide Every Day," http://opinion.inquirer.net/95929/seven-filipinos-commit-suicide-every-day#ixzz-5JryBo1qk, accessed June 29, 2018.

> 7. Les Parrott III, *Helping the Struggling Adolescent: A Guide to Thirty Common Problems for Parents, Counselors, & Youth Workers* (Grand Rapids: Zondervan, 1993), 308–309.
> 8. Joseph Too Shao and Rosa Ching Shao, *Ezra & Nehemiah*, 93–94.
> 9. Donald L. Nathanson, *Shame and Pride: Affect, Sex, and the Birth of Self* (New York: Norton, 1992), 58.
> 10. Melody Beattie, "Brainy Quote," https://www.brainyquote.com/authors/melody_beattie?img=null, accessed July 2, 2018.
> 11. Jeffrey A. Kottler and David S. Shepard, *Introduction to Counseling: Voices from the Field* (Stamford, CT: Cengage Learning, 2015), 226.

The concluding word from God shows that the story of Jonah is really a didactic narrative – a story whose purpose is to teach God's truth. The Lord God does not condemn Jonah to despair, death, or even damnation. Caringly, compellingly, God rebukes Jonah: "You have been concerned about this plant, though you did not tend it or make it grow. It sprang up overnight and died overnight" (4:10). God uses the illustration of his care of a mere plant to show Jonah how greatly he cared for the "more than a hundred and twenty thousand people" of Nineveh (4:11b). He invites Jonah to carefully consider this illustration. On one side is Jonah with the vine plant he so loves; on the other is God with the Ninevites. Jonah is deeply troubled by a dying vine plant that he has done nothing to nurture. On the other hand, God presents the relationship between the Lord and the Ninevites as that of a father and his children, as well that of the Creator and his creatures, including even the animals. Jonah's vine existed for a mere twenty-four hours. The relationship between God and the inhabitants of Nineveh, however, is of a much longer duration and more intense. If the withering of the plant caused Jonah such suffering that he sought to die, how much more hurtful and heartrending would God find the destruction of Nineveh "in which there are more than a hundred and twenty thousand people who cannot tell their right hand from their left – and also many animals" (4:11b)?

The main thrust of God's argument is this: If Jonah's distress over the demise of the plant is legitimate, then does not the Lord God's distress over the potential destruction of Nineveh have greater legitimacy? The phrase "who cannot tell their right hand from their left" is an idiom for being morally and spiritually unaware. It could also refer to the entire population. The final phrase, "and also many animals," is a strange expression. The underlying argument could be: If Jonah will not allow God to have compassion on Nineveh for the sake of the one hundred and twenty thousand people he created and cared for, will he allow God to have compassion on Nineveh for the sake of the animals, because, after all, Jonah did have compassion on a plant for whose growth he did nothing?

In contrast to the classical prophets and their oracles, the book of Jonah ends with God speaking and teaching one self-centered prophet about his heart for all people – his loving concern and compassion not just for the Israelites, not just for the Ninevites, but also for Jonah, and for all who would one day read the book of Jonah.

We see God's patience in action in his long-suffering tolerance of his stubborn prophet Jonah. The challenge for many in leadership is bringing people to get things done. God, however, is more interested in the servant-like character of his messenger. The Lord as the God of heaven, who made the sea and the dry land, treasures relationship with his people over their accomplishments. This is transformational servant leadership – mobilizing all members in the organization to make conscious decisions about where each needs to be and to become, and the role each needs to play in the system. In this model, the leader works alongside the people, or even from the rear, offering encouragement and support as members gather around ideas and opportunities of their own making – all in pursuit of a common purpose.[28]

The book of Jonah closes with this question: "And should I not have concern for the great city of Nineveh, in which there are more than a hundred and twenty thousand people who cannot tell their right hand from their left – and also many animals?" (4:11). The abruptness of the book's closing is intentional, highlighting Jonah's disciplined silence! It is a forceful conclusion, pointing to the now humbled Jonah, who no longer fights or finds faults with God's ways. No longer does he voice his anger against the universality of God's grace. Will you, the reader, agree with an audible "Amen!"?

---

28. Gary V. Nelson and Peter M. Dickens, *Leading in Disorienting Times: Navigating Church & Organizational Change* (Canada: TCP, 2015), 149.

SELECTED BIBLIOGRAPHY

Aier, Akumsungla. "Relationship of Object Relations, Shame and Narcissism to Adolescents' False Self Behavior on Social Network Sites." EdD diss., Asia Graduate School of Theology, Philippines, 2018.

Arnold, Daniel. *Wrestling with God: Commentary on the Book of Jonah*. San Bernardino, CA: CreateSpace, 2014. Originally published as *Jonah: Bras de fer avec un Dieu de grâce*. Saint-Légier, Switzerland: Editions Emmaüs, 2004.

Barrett, Rob. "Meaning More than They Say." *Journal of the Study of the Old Testament* 37, no. 2 (2012): 245. Online: http://www.sagepub.co.uk/journalsPermissions.nav, DOI:10.11.77/0309089212466464. Accessed August 5, 2016.

Beattie, Melody. "Brainy Quote." Online: https://www.brainyquote.com/quotes/melody_beattie_134462. Accessed February 16, 2018.

Belser, Jordan. "The Traumatized Child: Implications for the Church in the Story of Mephibosheth." *JAM* 19, no. 1 (2018): 71–95.

Bosma, Carl J. "Jonah 1:9 – An Example of Elenctic Testimony." *CTJ* 48 (2013): 65–90.

Burke, Daniel. "Billy Graham, Whose 'Matchless Voice Changed the Lives of Millions,' Dies at 99." Online: https://www.cnn.com/2018/02/21/us/billy-graham-obit/index.html. Accessed February 21, 2018.

Butuyan, Joel Ruiz. "Seven Filipinos Commit Suicide Every Day." Online: http://opinion.inquirer.net/95929/seven-filipinos-commit-suicide-every-day#ixzz5JryBo1qk. Accessed June 29, 2018.

Ching, Rosa S. "An Analytical Key and Exegetical Commentary on the Book of Jonah." MA thesis, Biblical Seminary of the Philippines, 1980.

Clarke, Sathianathan. "The Task, Method and Content of Asian Theologies." *Asian Theology on the Way: Christianity, Culture and Context*, ch 1. Edited by Peniel Jesudason Rufus Rajkumar. London: SPCK, 2012.

Clinton, Tim, and Ron Hawkins. *The Quick-Reference Guide to Biblical Counseling*. Grand Rapids: Baker Books, 2009.

Crouch, Andy. "The Return of Shame." *Christianity Today* (March 2015): 32–41.

Drane, John. *Introducing the Old Testament*. 3rd edition. Oxford: Lion Hudson, 2011.

Forti, Tova. "Of Ships and Seas, and Fish and Beasts: Viewing the Concept of Universal Providence in the Book of Jonah through the Prism of Psalms." *JSOT* 35, no. 3 (2011): 359–374.

Friedman, Vanessa. "Andy Spade on Kate's Death: 'There Was No Indication and No Warning.'" Online: https://www.nytimes.com/2018/06/06/style/kate-spade-husband-andy-spade.html. Accessed June 29, 2018.

Georges, Jayson. "Why Has Nobody Told Me This Before? The Gospel the World Is Waiting For." *Mission Frontiers* (Jan–Feb 2015): 7–10.

Hagee, John. Online: https://www.facebook.com/JohnHageeMinistries/photos/a.../10152523551927518/. Accessed February 16, 2018.

Hendin, Herbert, Lakshmi Vijayuakumar, José M. Bertolote, Hong Wang, Michael R. Phillips, and Jane Pirkis. "Epidemiology of Suicide in Asia." Online: https://www.who.int/mental_health/resources/suicide_prevention_asia_chapter1.pdf?ua1. Accessed May 11, 2019.

Hess, Richard S. *The Old Testament: A Historical, Theological, and Critical Introduction*. Grand Rapids: Baker Academic, 2016.

Iong, Ma Man, "Shall God Not Also Pity . . .? Relational Divine Mission on the Book of Jonah from the Perspective of Genesis 1–3." MA Thesis, Luther Seminary, 2013.

Kaufman, Gershen. *Shame: The Power of Caring*, 3rd edition. Rochester: Schenkman Books, 1992.

Laan, Ray Vander. "That the World May Know." Online: https://www.thattheworldmayknow.com/assyrians/. Accessed November 4, 2017.

McLeod, Saul. "Obedience to Authority." Online: https://www.simplypsychology.org/obedience.html. Accessed December 1, 2018.

———. "The Milgram Shock Experience," Online: https://www.simplypsychology.org/milgram.html. Accessed April 18, 2019.

Mark, Joshua J. "Nineveh: Definition." *Ancient History Encyclopedia*. Online: https://www.ancient.eu/nineveh/. Accessed November 6, 2017.

Martel, Janelle, and Erica Cirino. "Passive Aggressive Personality." Online: https://www.healthline.com/health/passive-aggressive-personality-disorder. Accessed March 4, 2016.

Moberly, R. W. L. "Educating Jonah." In *Old Testament Theology: Reading the Hebrew Bible as Christian Scripture*, 181–210. Grand Rapids: Baker Academic, 2013.

Morris, Henry M. *The Remarkable Journey of Jonah: A Scholarly, Conservative Study of His Amazing Record*. Green Forest, AR: Master Books, 2003.

Nathanson, Donald L. *Shame and Pride: Affect, Sex, and the Birth of Self*. New York: W. W. Norton & Co., 1992.

"Nasaan Kaya Ako – Papuri Singer." Online: https://www.youtube.com/watch?v=48s9bfGMIPc. Accessed July 12, 2018.

Nelson, Gary V., and Peter M. Dickens. *Leading in Disorienting Times: Navigating Church & Organizational Change*. Canada: TCP, 2015.

Nixon, Rosemary. *The Message of Jonah: Presence in the Storm*. Bible Speaks Today Series. Edited by J. A. Motyer. Downers Grove, IL: IVP Academic, 2003.

Selected Bibliography

Parrott III, Les. *Helping the Struggling Adolescent: A Guide to Thirty Common Problems for Parents, Counselors, & Youth Workers.* Grand Rapids: Zondervan, 1993.

Perry, T. A. *The Honeymoon Is Over: Jonah's Argument with God.* Peabody: Hendrickson, 2006.

"Philippine Visayan Festivals: Dinagyang." *Adeline's Blog,* December 19, 2016. Online: http://www.adelinefilamfood.com/2016/12/19/philippine-visayan-festivals-dinagyang/. Accessed January 24, 2018.

Richardson, Carl H. *Catching Your Second Wind to Finish Well.* Tampa: Beyond Borders, 2011.

Ryu, Chesung Justin. "Silence as Resistance: A Postcolonial Reading of the Silence of Jonah in Jonah 4:1–11," *JSOT* 34, no. 2 (2009): 195–218.

Schellenberg, Annette. "An Anti-Prophet among the Prophets? On the Relationship of Jonah to Prophecy," *JSOT* 39 (2015): 353–371.

Shao, Joseph Too, and Rosa Ching Shao. *Ezra and Nehemiah.* ABC. Carlisle: Langham Global Library, 2019

———. *Joel, Nahum & Malachi.* ABC. Edited by Bruce J. Nicholls. Manila: Asia Theological Association, 2013.

Shao, Rosa Ching. "Anger Management or Mismanagement: When It Thunders, It Roars or Rolls." In *Expanding Horizons: Theological Reflections,* edited by Joseph T. Shao, Rosa C. Shao and Jean Uayan, 119–129. Valenzuela: Biblical Seminary of the Philippines, 2010.

———. "When Suicidal Thoughts Loom." In *BSOP in Focus* 103 (October–December 2018): 1–3.

Stacey, Aisha. "Prophet Jonah." Online: https://www.islamreligion.com/articles/2548/prophet-jonah/. Accessed June 15, 2018.

Stelter, Brian. "CNN's Anthony Bourdain Dead at 61." Online: https://edition.cnn.com/2018/06/08/us/anthony-bourdain-obit/index.html. Accessed June 29, 2018.

Strawn, Brent A. "On Vomiting: Leviticus, Jonah, Ea(a)rth." *CBQ* 74 (2012): 444–465.

Tan, P. L. "What Is the Difference between 'Fore-Telling" and 'Forth-Telling?'" Online: http://www.tanbible.com/tol_faq/faq_general_02.htm. Accessed April 11, 2018.

Tawfiq, Idris. "In the Belly of the Whale – The Story of Jonah." Online: http://aboutislam.net/reading-islam/understanding-islam/in-the-belly-of-the-whale-story-of-jonah/. Accessed June 15, 2018.

Tong, Daniel. *A Biblical Approach to Feng Shui & Divination.* Singapore: Genesis Books, 2006.

Villanueva, Federico. *Lamentations: A Pastoral and Contextual Commentary.* ABC. Carlisle: Langham Global Library, 2016.

———. "Preaching Lament." In *Reclaiming the Old Testament for Christian Preaching*, edited by Grenville J. R. Kent, Paul J. Kissling and Laurence A. Turner. Downers Grove: IVP Academic, 2010.

Vujicic, Nicolas James. *Be the Hands and Feet: Living Out God's Love for All His Children*. New York: WaterBrook, 2018.

Walton, John H. *Ancient Near Eastern Thought and the Old Testament: Introducing the Conceptual World of the Hebrew Bible*. 2nd edition. Grand Rapids: Baker Academic, 2018.

———. "Jonah." In *Zondervan Illustrated Bible Backgrounds Commentary*. Vol. 3. Edited by John H. Walton. Grand Rapids: Zondervan, 2009.

Wolff, H. W. *Obadiah and Jonah: A Commentary*. Minneapolis: Augsburg, 1986.

Wu, Xian Zhang. *You Don't Know My Heart: Commentary on the Book of Jonah*. Taipei, Taiwan: Taosheng Publishing House of Taiwan Lutheran Church, 2013.

Youngblood, Kevin J. "Jonah: God's Scandalous Mercy." In *Hearing the Message of Scripture: A Commentary on the Old Testament*, edited by Daniel I. Block. Grand Rapids: Zondervan, 2013.

Zachman, Randall C. *John Calvin as Teacher, Pastor, and Theologian: The Shape of His Writings and Thoughts*. Kindle edition. Grand Rapids: Baker Academic, 2006.

Asia Theological Association
54 Scout Madriñan St. Quezon City 1103, Philippines
Email: ataasia@gmail.com Telefax: (632) 410 0312

OUR MISSION
The Asia Theological Association (ATA) is a body of theological institutions, committed to evangelical faith and scholarship, networking together to serve the Church in equipping the people of God for the mission of the Lord Jesus Christ.

OUR COMMITMENT
The ATA is committed to serving its members in the development of evangelical, biblical theology by strengthening interaction, enhancing scholarship, promoting academic excellence, fostering spiritual and ministerial formation and mobilizing resources to fulfill God's global mission within diverse Asian cultures.

OUR TASK
Affirming our mission and commitment, ATA seeks to:

- **Strengthen** interaction through inter-institutional fellowship and programs, regional and continental activities, faculty and student exchange programs.
- **Enhance** scholarship through consultations, workshops, seminars, publications, and research fellowships.
- **Promote** academic excellence through accreditation standards, faculty and curriculum development.
- **Foster** spiritual and ministerial formation by providing mentor models, encouraging the development of ministerial skills and a Christian ethos.
- **Mobilize** resources through library development, information technology and infra-structural development.

To learn more about ATA, visit www.ataasia.com or facebook.com/AsiaTheologicalAssociation

Langham
PARTNERSHIP

Langham Literature, along with its publishing work, is a ministry of Langham Partnership.

Langham Partnership is a global fellowship working in pursuit of the vision God entrusted to its founder John Stott –

> *to facilitate the growth of the church in maturity and Christ-likeness through raising the standards of biblical preaching and teaching.*

Our vision is to see churches in the majority world equipped for mission and growing to maturity in Christ through the ministry of pastors and leaders who believe, teach and live by the Word of God.

Our mission is to strengthen the ministry of the Word of God through:
- nurturing national movements for biblical preaching
- fostering the creation and distribution of evangelical literature
- enhancing evangelical theological education

especially in countries where churches are under-resourced.

Our ministry

Langham Preaching partners with national leaders to nurture indigenous biblical preaching movements for pastors and lay preachers all around the world. With the support of a team of trainers from many countries, a multi-level programme of seminars provides practical training, and is followed by a programme for training local facilitators. Local preachers' groups and national and regional networks ensure continuity and ongoing development, seeking to build vigorous movements committed to Bible exposition.

Langham Literature provides majority world preachers, scholars and seminary libraries with evangelical books and electronic resources through publishing and distribution, grants and discounts. The programme also fosters the creation of indigenous evangelical books in many languages, through writer's grants, strengthening local evangelical publishing houses, and investment in major regional literature projects, such as one volume Bible commentaries like the *Africa Bible Commentary* and the *South Asia Bible Commentary*.

Langham Scholars provides financial support for evangelical doctoral students from the majority world so that, when they return home, they may train pastors and other Christian leaders with sound, biblical and theological teaching. This programme equips those who equip others. Langham Scholars also works in partnership with majority world seminaries in strengthening evangelical theological education. A growing number of Langham Scholars study in high quality doctoral programmes in the majority world itself. As well as teaching the next generation of pastors, graduated Langham Scholars exercise significant influence through their writing and leadership.

To learn more about Langham Partnership and the work we do visit **langham.org**

CPSIA information can be obtained
at www.ICGtesting.com
Printed in the USA
BVHW040956020819
554973BV00012B/292/P